Check Your
CHEMISTRY

Lt. Cdr A. P. Giddings, B.Sc., M.Ed., Royal Navy
Royal Naval Engineering College
Plymouth

and

J. S. Clarke, M.Sc., M.A., C.Chem., F.R.S.C.
Senior Science Master
Alleyn's School
London

HODDER AND STOUGHTON
LONDON SYDNEY AUCKLAND TORONTO

British Library Cataloguing in Publication Data

Giddings, A. P.
 Check your chemistry.
 1. Chemistry
 I. Title   II. Clarke, J. S.
 540   QD31.2

 ISBN 0 340 35218 3

First printed 1985

Typesetting by Macmillan India Ltd, Bangalore, India and Printed in Great
Britain for Hodder and Stoughton Educational a division of Hodder and
Stoughton Ltd Mill Road, Dunton Green, Sevenoaks, Kent, by
Richard Clay (The Chaucer Press) Ltd, Bungay, Suffolk.

Contents

Preface

These notes and revision questions are intended for use by students who are near the end of 16 + chemistry courses (G.C.E., C.S.E. or G.C.S.E.).

Most 16 + syllabuses can be broken down into the topics covered in the chapters of this book. For each topic there are some brief reminders of the basic facts and theories. The Periodic Table on page 121 may be generally useful.

The revision questions at the end of each chapter are of the following types:

1 **Multiple choice questions.** For each question, five alternative answers are suggested only one of which is correct. The letter of the correct alternative should be used as the response.
2 **Matching pairs questions.** Several possible answers are listed and they may be used once, several times, or not at all as the responses to the questions which follow. Again, there is only one correct alternative for each question, and the letter of this alternative should be used as the response.

Each test contains twenty-five or thirty questions, and students should aim to complete them in 30 to 45 minutes, which is the rate of working and checking required for examinations. The answers are to be found at the back of the book.

We hope that these notes and questions will prove useful for chemistry students. The following, also published by Hodder and Stoughton, may be consulted for further guidance:

Teach Yourself Chemistry, J. S. Clarke
A New Chemistry, S. Clynes, D. J. W. Williams and J. S. Clarke

A. P. Giddings
J. S. Clarke

1 Classification

Solids, Liquids and Gases

The phase of a substance under normal conditions of temperature and pressure is its physical state, which may be solid, liquid or gas.

The particles of an atomic or molecular solid are close together. The particles are held together by weak forces (van der Waals' forces) and sometimes this produces a regular arrangement of the particles and the resulting solid is crystalline. Other solids, such as polymers, contain a small number of very large particles (sometimes called macromolecules), and these are not obviously crystalline. A solid has a fixed shape and size at a fixed temperature.

In many liquids, the forces between particles are weaker, because the particles are further apart than in the solid phase, and the particles have some freedom of movement. The motion of liquid particles is random and zig-zag (Brownian Motion). A liquid has a fixed size at a fixed temperature but takes the shape of the base of its container. In gases the separation and motion of such particles causes the forces between particles to be almost negligible. Gas particles move (by diffusion) so that they completely fill their containers.

Provided that a substance does not undergo some chemical reaction, either alone or with the atmosphere, its phase can be changed by change of temperature. The temperature at which a solid becomes liquid is called the melting point (freezing point) and that at which a liquid changes into a gas is called the boiling point. Thus:

$$\text{solid} \underset{\textit{freezing}}{\overset{\textit{melting}}{\rightleftarrows}} \text{liquid} \underset{\textit{condensation}}{\overset{\textit{boiling}}{\rightleftarrows}} \text{gas}$$

Increasing the temperature of solids, liquids and gases causes an increase in volume (expansion) to occur. Pressure changes will also change the volume of gases, and decreasing the pressure on

1

a liquid may cause it to boil without heating. Pressure changes
have little effect on solids.

Elements, Compounds and Mixtures

When a pure chemical substance contains only one kind of
atom, it is called an element, and it cannot be split into simpler
substances by chemical means. Many of the elements, such as
sulphur, carbon and oxygen, occur naturally, while others, such
as californium (98) and nobelium (102), are synthetic. All of
the elements are shown in the Periodic Table (found on page
121.)

Elements like sodium, potassium and fluorine are never
found naturally occurring as elements. They react very readily
with substances like oxygen and water that are found in the air
or on the earth's surface. When a substance contains atoms of
two or more different elements, combined chemically, it is
known as a compound. Sodium chloride (NaCl) for example
contains sodium and chlorine atoms chemically combined.

Most chemicals do not occur naturally as pure substances,
but as mixtures. Air is a mixture of various gases, and the sea is
water with various salts dissolved in it. Mixtures have no fixed
and constant composition, and have no chemical bonding
between the constituents. The properties of mixtures are
generally those of their components. Pure solids and liquids can
be distinguished from mixtures because the presence of
impurities usually lowers the melting point and raises the
boiling point of pure substances.

Separation Techniques

Elements and compounds rarely occur in a high state of purity
in nature. The following are techniques used in the laboratory
to separate the components of mixtures, and the same processes
will be found, on a large scale, in industry.

1   **Solvent extraction.** A liquid (solvent) is chosen that will
    dissolve part but not all of the mixture, so that part of the
    mixture will be in the form of a solution and the other
    part a solid residue. The substance that dissolves is called
    the solute. Polar solvents (e.g. water) generally dissolve

ionic compounds. Non-polar solvents (e.g. methylbenzene) generally dissolve covalent compounds.

2 **Filtration** separates an insoluble residue from a liquid or solution. The insoluble solid (precipitate) remains on the filter paper, and may be washed and dried to purify it further. The liquid passing through the filter paper is called the filtrate. An insoluble solid and a liquid or solution mixture may also be separated by centrifuging. In this process the solid goes to the bottom of the tube, and the liquid or solution can be removed by using a pipette or by decantation (pouring it off).

3 **Evaporation.** Providing that a solute does not undergo thermal decomposition at a temperature below the boiling point of a solvent, the solvent may be removed by boiling it away.

If well-formed crystals are required the evaporation must take place slowly once a saturated solution has been produced. Crystals will be formed in a mother liquor. Different solids have different solubilities in the same solvent, and so upon crystallization the least soluble solute will separate out first.

If the solvent in a solution is boiled off, condensed on a cold surface and collected, the process is called distillation and the liquid collected is the distillate. This process when carried out at reduced pressure will cause the solvent to boil at a temperature below its normal boiling point. Different liquids at the same pressure have different boiling points, so the distillation of a mixture of liquids (fractional distillation) will produce the most volatile component (lowest boiling point) as the first distillate.

4 **Sublimation.** When a solid on heating is converted directly into a gas without passing through an observable liquid phase, and then on cooling the gas solidifies, it is said to sublime. Common examples of substances that undergo sublimation under normal conditions are many ammonium salts (e.g. ammonium carbonate used in smelling salts), iodine (produces a purple vapour) and solid carbon dioxide (dry ice).

5 **Chromatography.** This technique can be used to separate a mixture of solutes. Each solute has a different solubility in a solvent and it will thus be moved a different distance through a stationary medium such as a filter paper

or aluminium oxide. The most soluble solute will move the furthest and insoluble substances will not move at all. Colourless solutes can be developed (using locating agents) so that they may be detected.

Questions

1   To separate an insoluble solid from a liquid the *best* technique would be

   A   evaporation.
   B   crystallization.
   C   filtration or centrifugation.
   D   distillation.
   E   sublimation.

2   To obtain sulphur from a mixture of sulphur and zinc the *best* solvent would be

   A   water.
   B   dilute sodium hydroxide solution.
   C   carbon disulphide.
   D   dilute sulphuric acid.
   E   ethanol.

3   Which of the following is *not* true of mixtures?

   A   fixed composition by mass
   B   separated by physical means
   C   small or zero heat change upon formation
   D   colour which is usually an average of the parts
   E   the mass is the sum of the separate masses

4   Which of the following mixtures *cannot* be separated completely by fractional distillation?

   A   water and ethanol
   B   butane and pentane
   C   oxygen and nitrogen
   D   sodium chloride and water
   E   sand and water

5 If a definite proportion of salt is dissolved in water the freezing point of the water is

  A increased.
  B decreased.
  C unaltered.
  D not predictable.
  E variable.

6 Which of the following chemicals can be purified by recrystallization from water?

  A silver chloride
  B barium sulphate
  C copper(II) sulphate
  D calcium carbonate
  E iron(II) hydroxide

7 Which of the following elements is too reactive to be found native (i.e. as an element) in the earth's crust or in the sea or in the air?

  A carbon
  B argon
  C copper
  D nitrogen
  E iodine

8 A substance that splits up on heating into parts which recombine on cooling is said to undergo

  A thermal dissociation.
  B thermal decomposition.
  C ionization.
  D sublimation.
  E distillation.

9 If a definite proportion of salt is dissolved in water the boiling point of the water is

  A increased.
  B decreased.
  C unaltered.
  D not predictable.
  E variable.

10   Which solid substance does *not* sublime on heating?

    A   carbon dioxide
    B   aluminium chloride
    C   iodine
    D   sodium chloride
    E   iron(III) chloride

Select the appropriate response from the following for *questions 11—15*.

    A   element
    B   compound
    C   mixture
    D   amalgam
    E   alloy

Which of these responses *best* describes

11   nichrome?

12   sodium dissolved in mercury?

13   steel?

14   sea water?

15   methane?

16   Terylene is *best* described as a

    A   polymeric substance.
    B   solid compound.
    C   liquid crystal.
    D   solid mixture.
    E   crystalline substance.

17   Which of the following techniques would be the most appropriate for the separation of the simple indicators in a universal indicator?

    A   chromatography
    B   distillation
    C   crystallization
    D   evaporation
    E   sublimation

18 Which of the following substances is *not* an element?

    A   copper
    B   zinc
    C   tin
    D   lead
    E   brass

19 Which of the following would be the *best* method of separating ammonium chloride from a mixture of ammonium chloride and sodium chloride?

    A   filtration
    B   sublimation
    C   decantation
    D   distillation
    E   chemical methods

20 When finely-divided forms of rhombic sulphur and hydrated copper(II) sulphate are mixed together, the colour of the resulting solid is

    A   pale blue.
    B   pale green.
    C   pale yellow.
    D   white.
    E   pale blue-yellow.

Select the appropriate response from the following for *questions 21–25*.

    A   polymeric substance
    B   solid element
    C   liquid element
    D   gaseous mixture
    E   crystalline substance

Which of these responses *best* describes

21 mercury?

22 rhombic sulphur?

23 nylon?

24 air?

25 bromine?

Select the appropriate response from the following for *questions 26—30.*

A fractional distillation
B chromatography
C filtration
D crystallization
E diffusion

Which of these responses *best* describes the separation of

26 naphtha from crude oil?

27 pieces of cork from dilute sulphuric acid?

28 the gases from liquid air?

29 copper(II) sulphate from its aqueous solution?

30 sulphur from its solution in methylbenzene (toluene)?

2 The Structure of Atoms

Sub-atomic Particles

An element is a substance which cannot be split into simpler substances by chemical means. The smallest possible particle of an element that can exist is called an atom. All the atoms of a particular element are chemically identical and chemically different from the atoms of all other elements.

At the centre of every atom is a nucleus which contains particles called nucleons. The most important nucleons are protons which are positively charged, and neutrons which have the same masses as protons but no charges. Outside the nucleus are negatively charged electrons which each have a mass $1/1837$ of that of a proton or a neutron and are responsible for chemical bonding. The electrons are arranged in energy levels or shells. The influence of the nucleus on electrons is less for those in the outer energy levels than for those situated close to the nucleus.

Electronic Configurations

The electronic configuration (structure) of its atoms is a good guide to the vigour and type of reaction of an element. The electronic configurations of some common elements are:

H							He
1							2
Li	Be	B	C	N	O	F	Ne
2, 1	2, 2	2, 3	2, 4	2, 5	2, 6	2, 7	2, 8
Na	Mg	Al	Si	P	S	Cl	Ar
2, 8, 1	2, 8, 2	2, 8, 3	2, 8, 4	2, 8, 5	2, 8, 6	2, 8, 7	2, 8, 8
K	Ca						
2, 8, 8, 1	2, 8, 8, 2						

Elements with a few electrons in the outermost shell are reactive metals. The noble gases are unreactive and we must conclude that their electronic configurations are stable ones.

Elements which are a few electrons short of the noble gas electronic configurations are reactive non-metals. The elements in the 'middle' of the Periodic Table are close to, or on the boundary between, metals and non-metals; they are less reactive than the elements in Groups I and VII, II and VI, etc.

The electrons in the various energy levels around the nucleus of an atom of an element are often shown in diagrams as circles but this is a matter of convenience. For a metal, the further the outer (valency) electrons are away from the nucleus the more reactive the element is. For a non-metal, the nearer the outer electrons are to the nucleus the more reactive the element is.

Atomic Number and Mass Number

Each element has a distinct number of protons in its nucleus called the atomic number (Z).

The atom is electrically neutral so the atomic number is also the number of electrons in that neutral atom.

The mass number (A) of an atom is the total number of protons and neutrons in the nucleus of the atom. Two atoms may be chemically identical because they both have the same number of protons (and electrons) but may have different numbers of neutrons and thus different masses. Hydrogen (in the form of 'protium') for example, has one proton and no neutrons in its neutral atom, and deuterium has one proton and one neutron. These two forms (nuclides) of the same element differ in mass number but have the same atomic number and are called isotopes.

Chemical Symbols

A symbol is used to represent one atom of an element. The symbol for a nuclide X is shown as $^4_Z X$. Thus hydrogen in the form of protium would be shown as $^1_1 H$, while deuterium (heavy hydrogen, D) would be shown as $^2_1 H$. Knowing the values of Z and A tells a scientist the numbers of all the sub-atomic particles in the neutral atom, and the information can be used to predict how that element will behave chemically and physically. Hydrogen, as studied in the laboratory, is a mixture in constant proportions of the two isotopes so that its relative atomic mass is constant (1.008 to 4 significant figures).

Chemical Combination

Atoms, other than those of the noble gases, do not always exist naturally by themselves because they tend to combine with other atoms of the same or different elements.

The Periodic Table gives the chemist an indication of the way in which atoms will behave chemically. The noble gases are presumably unreactive because of the arrangements of their electrons. They have stable electronic configurations. When atoms combine the electrons in the outer energy levels are transferred or shared in order to achieve these electronic configurations (see page 9), and ions or molecules are produced respectively.

Equations

Chemical reactions can be expressed in terms of the number of atoms, molecules and/or ions by means of equations. The left-hand side shows the substances reacting, or the reactants (reagents), and the right-hand side of the arrow indicates what is produced (the products).

The symbols (s) = solid, (l) = liquid, (g) = gas, (aq) = aqueous solution, may be used to indicate the physical state of the reactants and products under standard thermochemical conditions of temperature (25 °C) and pressure (10^5 Pa).

Balanced equations also indicate the relative numbers of atoms/molecules of reactants and products involved in the reaction. If the relative atomic/molecular masses are considered in grams they are called molar masses (see page 52). For example

$$Fe(s) \ + \ S(s) \quad \rightarrow \quad FeS(s)$$

where the molar masses are

$$56 \, g \qquad 32 \, g \qquad \qquad 88 \, g$$

and $C_2H_4(g) \ + \ 3O_2(g) \ \rightarrow \quad 2CO_2(g) + 2H_2O(l)$

By Avogadro's Law (applicable to gases only)

$$1 \text{ vol.} \qquad 3 \text{ vol.} \qquad \quad 2 \text{ vol.} \qquad (2 \times 18 \, g)$$

Where 1 molar volume is 22.4 dm^3 under the standard conditions for gases (usually 0°C and 1.013 × 10^5 Pa).

Questions

1 Which of the following particles is a cation?

	electrons	protons	neutrons
A	6	6	6
B	1	1	2
C	18	17	18
D	18	20	20
E	11	11	12

2 Which of the following particles has a mass number of 24?

	electrons	protons	neutrons
A	12	11	12
B	12	12	12
C	12	13	12
D	10	13	14
E	12	12	13

3 A particle which contains 8 protons, 8 neutrons and 10 electrons is

A an atom.
B a cation.
C an anion.
D a polymer.
E radioactive.

4 Which of the following particles is an atom?

	electrons	protons	neutrons
A	18	16	16
B	18	17	18
C	18	18	22
D	18	19	21
E	18	20	20

5 Which of the following particles has an atomic number of 10?

	electrons	protons	neutrons
A	5	5	5
B	4	4	6
C	9	10	12
D	10	11	12
E	9	9	10

6   Nuclides belonging to the same element have the same number of

    A   neutrons.
    B   protons.
    C   neutrons + protons.
    D   isotopes.
    E   allotropes.

7   Which is the most reactive metal in Group I?

    A   lithium $(Z = 3)$

    B   sodium $(Z = 11)$

    C   potassium $(Z = 19)$

    D   rubidium $(Z = 37)$

    E   caesium $(Z = 87)$

8   Which of the following (in the nucleus of one atom of the element) gives the atomic number of an element?

    A   electrons
    B   neutrons
    C   protons
    D   mesons
    E   neutrinos

9   Isotopes of an element have the same number of

    A   protons.
    B   protons + neutrons.
    C   neutrons.
    D   electrons + neutrons.
    E   nucleons.

10   All of the elements in the same group in the Periodic Table have the same

    A   relative atomic mass.
    B   total number of electrons.
    C   mass number.
    D   number of outer electrons.
    E   atomic number.

11 Which is the most reactive non-metal in Group VII?

    A   fluorine $(Z = 9)$
    B   chlorine $(Z = 17)$
    C   bromine $(Z = 35)$
    D   iodine $(Z = 53)$
    E   astatine $(Z = 85)$

12 Which of the following electronic structures is that of a metal?

    A   2
    B   2, 4
    C   2, 7
    D   2, 8
    E   2, 8, 2

13 In order to become a fluorine atom, a fluoride ion must

    A   gain an electron.
    B   gain more than one electron.
    C   lose an electron.
    D   lose more than one electron.
    E   gain a proton.

14 An element has an atomic number of 6. It would be expected
    to have similar physical and chemical properties to an element
    of atomic number

    A   4.
    B   8.
    C   12.
    D   14.
    E   16.

15 An element, E, consists of two isotopes (nuclides). The
    proportions are 70% of ^{63}E and 30% of ^{65}E. Which one of
    the following is the relative atomic mass of E?

    A   63.3
    B   63.6
    C   64.0
    D   64.3
    E   64.7

Select the appropriate response from the following for *questions 16-20*.

   A   silicon
   B   chlorine
   C   potassium
   D   neon
   E   aluminium

Which of these elements has the following properties?

16   a very reactive metal

17   an element that is rather unreactive in the laboratory but its compounds are widespread and abundant

18   a structural metal having good corrosion resistance

19   an unreactive gas

20   a very reactive non-metal

The responses A to E listed below for *questions 21-25* are the atomic numbers of five pairs of elements.

   A   2 and 18
   B   3 and 19
   C   5 and 7
   D   6 and 16
   E   9 and 17

Which of these responses *best* describes a pair of elements which

21   are both unreactive?

22   are members of the same period in the Periodic Table?

23   are reactive non-metals?

24   both exist in allotropic forms?

25   are successive members of the same group in the Periodic Table?

3 Bonding and Structure

Ionic Bonding

The noble gases are unreactive because they have very stable electronic configurations (structures). When a neutral atom has an electronic configuration close to that of a noble gas, it may form compounds by the gain or the loss of electrons. The species formed are called ions. These ions retain the original nuclei, but are charged because in each ion the number of protons is no longer equal to the number of electrons.

For example, a sodium atom has one electron more than a neon atom. In compound formation one electron is lost by transfer and an ion with a single positive charge (a cation) results.

$$Na \rightarrow Na^+ + e^-$$

Similarly a chlorine atom has one electron fewer than an argon atom and will attain the stable electronic configuration of argon by gaining one electron. The resulting chloride ion is negatively charged (an anion).

$$Cl + e^- \rightarrow Cl^-$$

When electrons are transferred from an electropositive atom like sodium to an electronegative atom like chlorine, ions are produced. The bonding between ions is called ionic or electrovalent bonding.

The elements in Group I of the Periodic Table produce ions with single positive charges, whereas Group II elements produce ions with double positive charges and Group III elements form ions with three positive charges. For example:

$$Ca \rightarrow Ca^{2+} + 2e^-$$
$$Al \rightarrow Al^{3+} + 3e^-$$

Conversely, elements in Group VII of the Periodic Table produce ions with single negative charges, Group VI elements produce ions with double negative charges and the Group V elements may produce ions with three positive charges. For example:

$$O + 2e^- \rightarrow O^{2-} \quad \text{(oxide ion)}$$
$$N + 3e^- \rightarrow N^{3-} \quad \text{(nitride ion)}$$

Covalent Bonding

Carbon will not form the C^{4+} or C^{4-} ion. This would require too much energy. One electron may be removed quite easily from a neutral species, but it becomes increasingly more difficult to remove electrons from species that have one or two positive charges. The same argument applies to the addition of electrons to a species that already has one or more negative charges. Atoms of elements like carbon form bonds by sharing electrons. The resultant species are called molecules, and the type of bond is called a covalent bond. Covalent bonding will be evident when elements in the centre of the Periodic Table combine, or when the difference in electronegative character of the atoms is small, i.e. they are close together in the Periodic Table. Atoms of the non-metals form molecules by covalent bonding, e.g. H_2, Cl_2 and I_2.

Hydrogen and chlorine atoms combine to produce hydrogen chloride molecules in which two electrons are shared between the atoms:

$$H^{\circ} \quad \text{and} \quad {}^{\times}_{\times}\text{Cl}^{\times\times}_{\times} \longrightarrow H^{\circ}_{\times}\text{Cl}^{\times\times\ \times}_{\times\times} $$

shared electrons

The resulting single covalent bond is often shown as a single line, thus hydrogen chloride is shown as $H-Cl$. The crosses and circles shown above represent electrons from the different atoms.

A covalent bond contains two electrons only. If more than two electrons are shared to attain the noble gas electronic configuration multiple bonds will be formed. For example:

$$ {}^{\times\ \times}_{\times}\text{O}^{\times} \quad \text{and} \quad {}^{\circ\ \circ}_{\circ}\text{O}^{\circ}_{\circ} \rightarrow {}^{\times\times}_{\times}\text{O}^{\times\ \circ\circ}_{\times\ \circ}\text{O}^{\circ}_{\circ} \quad \text{or} \quad O{=}O $$

and $\overset{\times}{\underset{\times}{\times}} \text{N} \times$ and $\overset{\circ}{\underset{\circ}{\circ}} \text{N} \overset{\circ}{\circ}$ → $\overset{\times}{\underset{\times}{\times}} \text{N} \overset{\times}{\underset{\circ}{\times}} \text{N} \overset{\circ}{\circ}$ or   N≡N

Pairs of electrons that are not involved in bonding are called lone pairs, and when both of the electrons in a covalent bond are donated by the same atom the bond is called a dative covalent bond or a co-ordinate linkage. Once formed, dative bonds are no different from other single covalent bonds. Both covalent and ionic bonding can exist in the same substance. For example, water and ammonia, both of which have lone pairs of electrons in their molecules, react together to produce some ammonium and hydroxide ions (the solution is better called aqueous ammonia than ammonium hydroxide).

$$\overset{\text{H}}{\underset{\text{H}}{\text{H} \times \text{N} \times}} \quad \text{and} \quad \overset{\text{H}}{\text{H} \overset{\times}{\circ} \text{O} \overset{\circ}{\circ}} \quad \rightarrow \quad \left[\overset{\text{H}}{\underset{\text{H}\uparrow}{\text{H} \times \text{N} \times \text{H}}} \right]^{+} \quad \text{and} \quad \left[\text{H} \overset{\circ\circ}{\underset{\times\circ}{\overset{\times}{\circ}\text{O}\overset{\times}{\circ}}} \right]^{-}$$

_   dative bond.

In this case, each atom retains the stable noble gas electronic configuration, but ions which contain covalent bonds have been produced. A dative bond may be indicated by an arrow showing the atom that has provided both of the electrons for the bond, e.g. the ammonium ion may be written

$$\left[\overset{\text{H}}{\underset{\text{H}}{\text{H}-\text{N} \rightarrow \text{H}}} \right]^{+}$$

Charges on Ions

Bonding involves only the electrons in the outer energy level of atoms, and the charge on an ion derived from an atom is related to the group number of the atom in the Periodic Table. Some common ions, with their charges, are listed in the tables on the next page.

Cations

1 +	2 +	3 +
hydrogen, H^+ potassium, K^+ silver, Ag^+ ammonium, NH_4^+	magnesium, Mg^{2+} calcium, Ca^{2+} zinc, Zn^{2+} lead (II), Pb^{2+} iron(II), Fe^{2+} copper(II), Cu^{2+}	aluminium, Al^{3+} iron(III), Fe^{3+}

Anions

1 −	2 −	3 −

chloride, Cl^-
bromide, Br^-
iodide, I^-
nitrate, NO_3^-
nitrite, NO_2^-
manganate(VII),
  MnO_4^-
hydroxide, OH^-
hydrogencarbonate,
  HCO_3^-
ethanoate, CH_3COO^-
(acetate)
	oxide, O^{2-}
	sulphate, SO_4^{2-}
	sulphite, SO_3^{2-}
	sulphide, S^{2-}
	thiosulphate, $S_2O_3^{2-}$
	carbonate, CO_3^{2-}
	dichromate, $Cr_2O_7^{2-}$
	ethanedioate,
	  $C_2O_4^{2-}$ (oxalate)
		phosphide, P^{3-}
		nitride, N^{3-}
		phosphate,
		  PO_4^{3-}

Macromolecules

Carbon atoms have the ability to form covalent bonds with other carbon atoms, resulting in long chains or rings. In the elemental state, if the atoms are arranged in the form of tetrahedra (each carbon atom being linked to four others in a regular three-dimensional arrangement), the diamond structure results. If, however, the atoms are linked in hexagons, the planar structure of graphite results. Both of these crystalline forms of carbon contain only carbon atoms, and are called allotropes of carbon.

[Other examples of elements that can exist in allotropic forms are sulphur (as rhombic and monoclinic forms) and oxygen as oxygen (O_2) and ozone (trioxygen, O_3). Oxygen and ozone differ in atomicity, i.e. the number of atoms in the molecule. Some metals, such as iron, also exist in allotropic forms which differ in physical properties due to the difference in structure between the forms.]

Poly(ethene) is an example of a carbon compound which contains a long chain of carbon atoms. Such large molecules are called polymers or macromolecules. Another common polymer is poly(chloroethene), often known as pvc.

$$\left[\begin{array}{cc} H & H \\ | & | \\ -C & -C- \\ | & | \\ H & H \end{array}\right]_n \qquad \left[\begin{array}{cc} H & H \\ | & | \\ -C & -C- \\ | & | \\ H & Cl \end{array}\right]_x$$

Poly(ethene)   Poly(chloroethene)

Silicon dioxide (silica, sand) is another example of a macromolecule: it is a hard crystalline solid which has a giant structure. Each silicon atom is at the centre of a regular tetrahedron, and there is an oxygen atom between every two silicon atoms. SiO_2 is thus the empirical formula of this substance. Molecular formulae are meaningless for macromolecules because these molecules have a variety of chain lengths, etc.

Questions

1 The number of electrons in a double covalent bond is

   A 0
   B 1
   C 2
   D 3
   E 4

2 The particles that are responsible for chemical bonding are

   A protons.
   B neutrons.
   C nucleons.
   D electrons.
   E alpha.

3 Which of the following pairs of elements will unite to give a covalent compound?

   A sodium and chlorine
   B magnesium and oxygen
   C sodium and sulphur
   D carbon and oxygen
   E copper and zinc

4 Which of the following pairs of elements will unite to give an ionic compound?

   A potassium and chlorine
   B potassium and sodium
   C sulphur and chlorine
   D sodium and argon
   E copper and tin

5 The number of electrons involved in the bonding between the two atoms of a nitrogen molecule is

   A 2
   B 3
   C 4
   D 5
   E 6

6 The noble gases are unreactive because they

   A have the same number of electrons in the outermost shell.
   B are gases with low melting and boiling points.
   C have an atomicity of one.
   D do not form allotropes.
   E have very stable electronic configurations.

7 Which of the following descriptions is typical of a compound that contains no ions?

   A non-volatile and soluble in polar solvents
   B volatile and soluble in polar solvents
   C non-volatile and insoluble in non-polar solvents
   D volatile and soluble in non-polar solvents
   E non-volatile and soluble in non-polar solvents

8 Which of the following oxides could be described as 'macromolecular'?

   A   carbon monoxide
   B   silicon dioxide
   C   dinitrogen tetraoxide
   D   sulphur dioxide
   E   sulphur trioxide

9 Which of the following elements, represented by their atomic numbers would, on combination with the element fluorine, probably produce the compound with the strongest ionic bonding?

   A   3
   B   11
   C   19
   D   37
   E   55

10 Which of the following pairs of elements, represented by their atomic numbers, will *not* form simple ionic compounds?

   A   6 and 17
   B   8 and 20
   C   9 and 13
   D   17 and 26
   E   17 and 55

11 Element M is in Group II of the Periodic Table and element T is in Group VII. Which one of the following represents the most likely formula of the compound formed between M and T?

   A M_2T_7

   B M_7T_2

   C M_2T

   D MT_2

   E   MT

Select the appropriate response from the following sets of atomic numbers for *questions 12—16*.

A   3, 11, 19, 37
B   5, 6, 7, 8
C   17, 35, 53, 85
D   41, 42, 44, 45
E   97, 98, 99, 100

Which of these responses *best* describes sets of elements which

12   are in the same short period?

13   are man-made?

14   are alkali metals?

15   are called 'halogens'?

16   form compounds that probably exist as coloured ions in aqueous solution?

Select the appropriate response, from the following list of ways in which chemical bonding can occur, for *questions 17—21*.

A   one atom transferring one electron to another atom
B   one atom transferring two electrons to another atom
C   one atom transferring two electrons, one to each of two other atoms
D   one atom receiving one electron from another atom
E   one atom receiving two electrons, one from each of two other atoms

Which of these responses *best* describes the following changes?

17   making sodium chloride from sodium and chlorine

18   converting a chlorine atom into a chloride ion

19   making calcium fluoride from calcium and fluorine

20   making sodium oxide from sodium and oxygen

21   making magnesium sulphide from magnesium and sulphur

22 Which of the following represents the simplest correct formula for potassium manganate(VII)?

A PMn_7
B $PMnO_4$
C KMg_7
D KMn_7
E $KMnO_4$

23 A metal, M, forms a sulphate, $M_2(SO_4)_3$. Which of the following is the correct formula for the corresponding chloride of M?

A MCl_3
B M_3Cl
C M_2Cl_3
D M_3Cl_2
E MCl_2

24 Which of the following elements may form ions having a charge of -2?

A   calcium
B   carbon
C   oxygen
D   helium
E   copper

25 An element has 12 protons and 12 neutrons in its nucleus. Which of the following statements is *not* correct?

A   Its atom has two electrons in the outermost shell.
B   Its atom has two electrons in the innermost shell.
C   It forms anions.
D   An atom of this element has a relative atomic mass of 24.
E   An atom of this element will resemble an atom of an element with an atomic number of 20.

4 The Periodic Table

The Structure of the Table

The Periodic Table is printed at the back of the book on page 121. The idea of a Periodic Table was established by Mendeléev (1869), who thought that relative atomic mass was the basic feature. The modern table contains more elements than were known in Mendeléev's time, and is based on atomic number.

If all the known elements are arranged in order of increasing atomic number a pattern, associated with the electronic structure of the elements, emerges. The table, in its usual form, consists of horizontal rows (periods), vertical columns (groups), and blocks of elements (such as the transition metals). It can be used to predict the way in which elements and their compounds will behave chemically and physically.

Periods

In each period the most metallic elements occur on the left-hand side, and the most non-metallic elements are found on the right. On the extreme right of each period is a noble gas. Across each period the maximum valency shown by elements in their common compounds usually rises. For example:

$$Na_2O ; MgO \; ; Al_2O_3 ; SiO_2 ; P_2O_5 ; SO_3 \quad ; (Cl_2O_7)$$
$$NaCl ; MgCl_2 ; AlCl_3 \; ; SiCl_4 ; PCl_5 \; ; (S_2Cl_2) ; \quad —$$

However, it may rise and then fall, as in the following series:

$$NaH; (MgH_2); (AlH_3); SiH_4; PH_3; H_2S; HCl$$

(The compounds in brackets are unstable).

Groups

All of the elements in the same main group in the table have the same number of electrons in their outer energy level (shell). They are similar in the form in which they occur in nature, the way in which they are manufactured, in their physical properties, chemical properties and uses. As the atomic number increases and the influence of the nucleus on the outer energy level electrons becomes less, there is an increase in the metallic character of main group elements. Note that some versions of the Periodic Table do not put hydrogen and, sometimes, helium in groups with the other elements. Hydrogen has some likenesses to the elements in both Groups I and VII, and helium is unlike the other noble gases because it has only two electrons in the atom. The noble gases are unreactive because they have very stable electronic configurations (structures).

Bond Formation

When metals are mixed the resulting mixture is called an alloy. When metals combine with non-metals they form ionic compounds in which the metal atoms become cations (positive ions), and the non-metal atoms become anions (negative ions). The metals are therefore reducing agents (because they are oxidized by the loss of one or more electrons), and the non-metals are oxidizing agents (because neutral atoms have gained one or more electrons). When elements that are close to each other in a period, such as two non-metals, combine, they do so by covalent bonding, i.e. sharing electrons, and molecules are produced.

The number of electrons gained, lost, or shared by an atom in compound formation is known as its valency (or oxidation number). The maximum valency shown by an element is often its group number, which is the number of electrons in the outermost energy level in the neutral atom. The individual ions or atoms of molecules produced in compound formation have the electronic configurations of the noble gases.

Group Characteristics

In *Group I* (the alkali metals) the sizes of the atoms and ions increase with increase in atomic number. The reactivity of the metals towards air and water increases likewise. The hydroxides and carbonates of these elements are usually stable to heat, and are soluble in water, producing alkaline solutions.

In *Group II* (the alkaline earth elements), as for Group I, the sizes of the atoms and ions, and the reactivity of the metals towards air and water, all increase with increasing atomic number. The hydroxides however, are less stable towards heat, and are 'insoluble' (magnesium hydroxide) or only slightly soluble (calcium hydroxide). The carbonates are less stable to heat (calcium carbonate decomposes in a kiln at 1100 °C) and are insoluble in pure water.

The *Group VII* elements are normally called the halogens, and in this group a graduation of properties with increase in atomic number can be clearly seen. Fluorine and chlorine are non-metallic gases at room temperature, bromine is a liquid, and iodine is a solid with a metallic lustre. Fluorine is a pale yellow-green in colour, chlorine is yellow-green, bromine red-brown and iodine is black (purple as a gas). The sizes of the atoms and ions increase with increase in atomic number. However, the oxidizing power of the elements decreases as the atomic number increases. Thus each halogen can displace those of greater atomic number from solutions of the latter's salts. The reactivity of the elements towards hydrogen and metals decreases with increase in atomic number.

The *d-block* elements, many or all of which are often called transition elements, are characterized by their high melting points and high densities. They exhibit many valencies, and in their compounds the hydrated ions often show characteristic colours, e.g. iron(II) sulphate, $FeSO_4 \cdot 7H_2O$, pale green; iron(III) chloride, $FeCl_3 \cdot 6H_2O$, yellow; copper(II) sulphate, $CuSO_4 \cdot 5H_2O$, blue.

Questions

1 Hydrogen is like many of the elements in Group VII in several respects *except* that

    A   it forms diatomic molecules.
    B   it is ionic in several compounds.
    C   there is room for one more electron in the outermost shell of the atom.
    D   it is a reducing agent.
    E   it may form an anion.

2 Which of the following electronic structures is that of a halogen?

    A   2, 8, 1
    B   2, 8, 2
    C   2, 8, 3
    D   2, 8, 7
    E   2, 8, 8

3 Hydrogen is like the elements in Group I because it

    A   has a low density.
    B   forms a small ion.
    C   forms covalent compounds.
    D   only forms cations.
    E   has one electron in the outermost shell.

4 Magnesium, calcium and barium are in the same group of the Periodic Table. It can therefore be predicted that barium will

    A   not react with cold water.
    B   be liberated at the cathode during the electrolysis of an aqueous solution of barium chloride.
    C   form an insoluble carbonate.
    D   form a very soluble hydroxide.
    E   form an amphoteric hydroxide.

5 Which of the following properties do the elements of a Group in the Periodic Table have in common?

    A   density
    B   atomic number
    C   number of electrons in the outermost shell
    D   reactivity
    E   relative atomic mass

6 In terms of chemical properties which of the following elements is the most non-metallic?

    A   carbon
    B   nitrogen
    C   oxygen
    D   fluorine
    E   neon

7 Which of the following sets of ions in Group I of the Periodic Table correctly gives these ions in order of increasing size?

A K^+, Li^+, Na^+
B Na^+, Li^+, K^+
C Li^+, Na^+, K^+
D Li^+, K^+, Na^+
E K^+, Na^+, Li^+

8 Which of the following is *not* a property of the elements in Group I?

A The size of the atom increases with increase in atomic number.
B The size of the ion increases with increase in atomic number.
C The reactivity of the element increases with increase in atomic number.
D The hydroxide of the element is insoluble in water.
E The carbonate of the element is usually stable to heat.

9 Which of the following formulae of chlorides could *not* be directly predicted from the position of the other element in the Periodic Table?

A KCl
B $CaCl_2$
C $AlCl_3$
D $PbCl_2$
E CCl_4

10 The element rubidium (Rb) is in Group I of the Periodic Table, and reacts vigorously with cold water forming rubidium hydroxide and hydrogen. Which of the following is the correct equation for this reaction?

A $2Rb + 2H_2O \rightarrow 2RbOH + H_2$
B $Rb + 2H_2O \rightarrow Rb(OH)_2 + H_2$
C $Rb + H_2O \rightarrow RbOH + H$
D $2Rb + 2H_2O \rightarrow 2RbO + 2H_2$
E $Rb + 3H_2O \rightarrow Rb(OH)_3 + 2H_2$

11 Which element has properties slightly out of step with the other four members of the following elements?

A lithium $(Z = 3)$
B sodium $(Z = 11)$
C potassium $(Z = 19)$
D rubidium $(Z = 37)$
E caesium $(Z = 87)$

12 Which of the following sets of symbols represent elements forming part of a Group in the Periodic Table?

A C   N   O   F
B Fe   Co   Ni   Cu
C F   Cl   Br   I
D Na   Mg   Al   Si
E H   He   Ne   Ag

13 The Periodic Table today is based on

A relative atomic mass.
B atomic number.
C atomic size.
D neutron number.
E isotopes.

14 In terms of chemical properties which of the following elements is the most metallic?

A neon
B sodium
C magnesium
D aluminium
E silicon

15 Which of the following properties is *not* that of a halogen (a Group VII element)?

A They are non-metallic.
B They are oxidizing agents.
C The oxidizing power increases with increase in atomic number.
D The colour deepens with increase in atomic number.
E They can all be obtained as gases.

Select the appropriate response from the following for *questions 16—20.*

A the metal with the lowest boiling point

B the metal which is most easily obtained from its oxide

C the metal which is obtained by the electrolysis of its oxide

D the metal which forms only one chloride, having the formula MCl_2

E the metal which is the main component of steel

Which of these responses *best* describes

16 sodium?

17 magnesium?

18 aluminium?

19 iron?

20 copper?

Select the appropriate response from the following list of elements for *questions 21—25.*

A sodium

B calcium

C chlorine

D iron

E copper

Which of these responses *best* describes

21 an element that forms a carbonate which is soluble in water?

22 a vigorous oxidizing agent?

23 an element which forms two sulphates with formulae MSO_4 and $M_2(SO_4)_3$?

24 an element that forms a hydride which is acidic in aqueous solution?

25 an element which is *not* made by electrolysis?

26 Which colour is not that of the crystalline substance indicated by the formula?

A $CuSO_4 \cdot 5H_2O$ – blue

B $FeSO_4 \cdot 7H_2O$ – pale green

C $FeCl_3 \cdot 6H_2O$ – yellow

D $KMnO_4$ – purple

E $CoCl_2 \cdot 6H_2O$ – white

27 Which of the following properties distinguishes an element in Group II from an element in Group I?

A The reactivity increases with an increase in atomic number.

B The hydroxide of the element is less stable to heat.

C The solubility of the hydroxide decreases with increase in atomic number of the element.

D The carbonate of the element is more stable to heat.

E The elements show variable valency.

28 Which of the following electronic structures is that of an alkali metal?

A 2, 1
B 2, 2
C 2, 3
D 2, 7
E 2, 8

29 Which of the following is not a property of a transition metal or its compounds but is a property of an alkali metal or its compounds?

A high density
B high melting point
C high boiling point
D many coloured compounds
E many soluble compounds

5 Redox Reactions

Oxidation and Reduction

Magnesium is said to be oxidized when it gains oxygen, forming magnesium oxide. In terms of electrons, each magnesium atom loses two electrons and each oxygen atom gains two electrons. Because it is oxidized magnesium is said to be a reducing agent, and because it is reduced oxygen is the oxidizing agent. The two processes are thus complementary, i.e. one cannot occur without the other. Metals in general are good reducing agents and are said to be electropositive because they form positive ions or cations. Non-metals are good oxidizing agents and are said to be electronegative because they form negative ions or anions.

Thus four definitions of oxidation are:

1   gain of oxygen by a substance;
2   an increase in the non-metallic constituent in a substance;
3   loss of hydrogen by a substance;
4   in terms of sub-atomic particles, the loss of electrons by a substance.

A codeword that is useful in remembering this fourth definition is 'oilrig'—oxidation is loss, reduction is gain (of electrons).

Electrolysis

The most powerful way of carrying out oxidation and reduction is by electrolysis. This may be done in aqueous solution, or using a molten (fused) substance. The substance through which electricity passes is called an electrolyte, and this substance must contain ions that are free to move if electrolysis is to occur.

The vessel in which electrolysis takes place is often called a voltameter. The electrolyte is linked to the electrical circuit via the anode and the cathode. Electricity (a flow of electrons) enters the electrolyte at the cathode and leaves by the anode.

During electrolysis anions migrate to the anode and oxidation occurs either because the anions lose electrons, or because the atoms of the anode itself lose electrons and are converted into cations. In the same way, cations migrate to the cathode and reduction occurs because the cations gain electrons.

Hydrogen is present as a cation in many aqueous solutions, as $H^+(aq)$, and hydrogen gas is often discharged or liberated during electrolysis at the cathode. The electrolysis of many aqueous solutions also produces oxygen, discharged at the anode. Hydrogen and oxygen thus appear to be chemical opposites, and this gives rise to another definition of oxidation, i.e. the loss of hydrogen by a species. For example, ammonia is said to be oxidized by hot copper(II) oxide to give nitrogen, steam and copper.

One mole of a singly charged ion reacts when 96 500 coulombs of electricity flow in a circuit. Thus:

$$Na^+ + e^- \rightarrow Na$$
$$96\,500\ C \quad 23\ g$$

and $\quad Cu^{2+} + 2e^- \rightarrow Cu$

$$2 \times 96\,500\ C \quad 64\ g$$

Some common examples of electrolysis are given in the following table:

Electrolyte	Products		Comments
	Cathode	*Anode*	
aluminium oxide	aluminium	oxygen	molten cryolite as solvent, graphite anode burns away
sodium chloride (molten)	sodium	chlorine	calcium chloride added, Downs' cell

Electrolyte	Products		Comments
	Cathode	*Anode*	
lead bromide (molten)	lead	bromine	
lead iodide (molten)	lead	iodine	
potassium iodide (molten)	potassium	iodine	
sodium chloride (in water)	hydrogen (if platinum or carbon (graphite) cathode)	chlorine	concentrated solution (see note)
copper sulphate (in water)	copper deposited	copper ions form	copper electrodes
sulphuric acid (dilute)	hydrogen (2 volumes)	oxygen (1 volume)	platinum electrodes

Note. When a concentrated aqueous solution of sodium chloride is electrolysed using a mercury cathode, sodium is produced and it dissolves in the mercury forming an amalgam. Hydrogen is produced only when the sodium amalgam runs into water.

The Electrochemical Series

Electrolytes are substances which, when in aqueous solution or fused (molten), are able to conduct electricity. The reactions that occur during electrolysis using direct current take place at the electrodes and only while the current flows.

Solid sodium chloride is not an electrolyte because in the solid state, the ions cannot move. When it is molten at $800\,^{\circ}C$

(or at a lower temperature if it is mixed with a flux such as calcium chloride), or when it is dissolved in water, and an electrical current is passed through it, the ions move to the appropriate electrodes. Ions are preferentially discharged at the electrodes according to the positions of the elements in the electrochemical or activity series. The order of some common elements in this series is:

Potassium
Calcium
Sodium
Magnesium
Aluminium
Zinc
Iron
Lead
Hydrogen, the standard element
Copper
Silver

There may be some departure from this series when the electrodes are inert or not of the metal appropriate to the cation, if the concentration is not the standard concentration of 1 mol dm^{-3} or if the temperature is not the standard thermochemical temperature of $25\,°C$.

Oxidizing and Reducing Agents

The ideas of reduction and oxidation (hence the name redox reactions) can be extended from elements to compounds. Common oxidizing agents are:

Oxygen (as in combustion) and other non-metals
Chlorine and sodium chlorate(I) (sodium hypochlorite)
Bromine
Hydrogen peroxide
Potassium manganate(VII) (turns from purple to colourless
    solution when reduced)
Potassium dichromate (turns from orange to green
    solution when reduced)
Nitric acid
Sulphuric acid
Other non-metals

Common reducing agents include:

Hydrogen
Carbon
Carbon monoxide
Sulphur dioxide
Potassium iodide
Metals
Iron(II) sulphate
Ammonia

Questions

1   The reaction of iron(II) chloride which occurs when
    chlorine is added is an example of

    A   oxidation.
    B   reduction.
    C   synthesis.
    D   hydrolysis.
    E   hydration.

2   Which of the following salts can react as a reducing agent
    in aqueous solution?

    A   sodium sulphite
    B   sodium nitrate
    C   sodium sulphate
    D   sodium hydrogencarbonate
    E   sodium chloride

3   Which of the following redox reactions does *not* involve a
    colour change?

    A   potassium manganate(VII) in acidic solution giving a
        solution containing manganese(II) ions
    B   sodium sulphite solution giving sodium sulphate
        solution
    C   potassium dichromate in acidic solution giving a
        solution containing chromium(III) ions
    D   iodine solution giving a solution containing iodide
        ions
    E   iron(III) ions giving iron(II) ions

4   Which of the following salts can react as an oxidizing
    agent in aqueous solution?

    A   sodium chloride
    B   sodium chlorate(I)
    C   sodium sulphide
    D   sodium sulphate
    E   sodium carbonate

5   The amount of electricity needed to give 1 mole of
    sodium in electrolysis is

    A $\frac{1}{3} \times 96\,500$ coulombs.
    B $\frac{1}{2} \times 96\,500$ coulombs.
    C $1 \times 96\,500$ coulombs.
    D $2 \times 96\,500$ coulombs.
    E $3 \times 96\,500$ coulombs.

6   Which of the following conversions is an example of
    reduction?

    A   chloride ions to chlorine atoms
    B   hydrogen atoms to hydrogen ions
    C   a metal to a metal sulphide
    D   sulphite ions to sulphate ions
    E   copper(II) ions to copper atoms

7   The conversion of an iron oxide to iron in a blast furnace
    is an example of

    A   oxidation.
    B   reduction.
    C   allotropy.
    D   isotopy.
    E   dehydration.

8   Which of the following sets of electrodes will give the
    greatest voltage when placed in a suitable electrolyte?

    A   two made of magnesium
    B   two made of copper
    C   two made of lead
    D   one of magnesium, one of copper
    E   one of lead, one of copper

9 What volume, in cm^3, of hydrogen will be produced at the cathode during the electrolysis of 'water' if the volume of oxygen produced is 20 cm^3?

A 10
B 20
C 30
D 40
E 80

10 Which of the following equations represents a redox reaction?

A $3NaOH + H_3PO_4 \rightarrow Na_3PO_4 + 3H_2O$

B $Ag^+(aq) + Cl^-(aq) \rightarrow AgCl(s)$

C $Fe(OH)_3 + 3HCl \rightarrow FeCl_3 + 3H_2O$

D $Ca(OH)_2 + CO_2 \rightarrow CaCO_3 + H_2O$

E $Mg(s) + 2H^+(aq) \rightarrow Mg^{2+}(aq) + H_2(g)$

11 During the electrolysis of concentrated hydrochloric acid between carbon(graphite) electrodes, 2 moles of chlorine are obtained at the anode. At the same time, at the cathode you would expect to obtain

A 1 mole of hydrogen.
B 2 moles of hydrogen.
C 1 mole of oxygen.
D 2 moles of oxygen.
E 1 mole of hydrogen + 1 mole of oxygen.

12 Which of the following electrolytes is used for the manufacture of sodium metal?

A aqueous sodium chloride
B aqueous sodium sulphate
C molten sodium chloride
D a molten mixture of sodium chloride and calcium chloride
E sodium oxide dissolved in cryolite

13 The particles which move in a metal wire when an electric current flows are called

   A   protons.
   B   neutrons.
   C   ions.
   D   electrons.
   E   electrolytes.

14 When an aqueous solution of copper(II) sulphate is electrolysed between copper electrodes

   A   copper is removed from the anode and deposited on the cathode.
   B   oxygen bubbles off at the anode and copper is deposited at the cathode.
   C   copper is deposited on the anode and hydrogen bubbles off at the cathode.
   D   copper is removed from the anode and oxygen bubbles off at the cathode.
   E   the copper(II) sulphate solution loses its colour.

15 Two voltameters are connected in series. When 2 moles of copper are obtained in one, the amount of silver (in moles) that will be obtained in the second will be

   A   1
   B   2
   C   3
   D   4
   E   6

Select the appropriate response from the following list of equations for *questions 16–20.*

   A $2Cl^- \rightarrow Cl_2 + 2e^-$

   B $2HNO_3 + Ca(OH)_2 \rightarrow Ca(NO_3)_2 + 2H_2O$

   C $2FeCl_2 + Cl_2 \rightarrow 2FeCl_3$

   D $Fe^{3+} + e^- \rightarrow Fe^{2+}$

   E $2FeCl_3 + Zn \rightarrow 2FeCl_2 + ZnCl_2$

Which of these responses *best* describes a reaction

16 in which reduction only has taken place?

17 that may happen at the anode during electrolysis?

18 in which neither oxidation nor reduction has taken place?

19 in which there is no colour change?

20 in which oxidation only has taken place?

Select the appropriate response from the following list of colour changes for *questions 21—25.*

    A   purple to colourless
    B   red to blue
    C   orange to green
    D   colourless to brown
    E   no colour change

Which of these responses *best* describes what would be observed when

21 potassium manganate(VII) behaves as an oxidizing agent?

22 potassium iodide is oxidized?

23 aqueous potassium hydroxide is neutralized by nitric acid?

24 potassium dichromate(VII) reacts with sulphur dioxide?

25 hydrogen peroxide reacts with sodium sulphite?

6 Acids, Bases and Salts

Definitions

An acid is a solution of a compound which contains H^+(aq) (hydrogen or oxonium ions) as the only positive ions. A base is a compound that will react with an acid to produce a salt plus water only. An aqueous solution of a soluble base is called an alkali, and contains hydroxide ions, OH^- (aq). A salt is the compound (other than water) produced when the hydrogen in an acid is wholly or partly replaced by a metal. In general terms

> an acid + a base → a salt + water

The removal of acidity or alkalinity from a solution is called neutralization, and may be represented in ionic terms by the equation

$$H^+(aq) + OH^-(aq) \rightarrow H_2O \text{ (l)}$$

Acidity

The degree of acidity of a substance depends on the concentration of hydrogen ions. Strong acids such as the mineral acids (sulphuric, hydrochloric and nitric acids) are almost totally dissociated in aqueous solution, whereas weak acids, such as carbonic acid, and organic acids are only partly dissociated. The degree of acidity is generally measured on a scale from 1 to 14 called the pH scale, which is a measure of the concentration of hydrogen ions.

A pH of 1 to 7 indicates acidity: hydrogen ions are in excess in the solution. An increase in pH here indicates a decrease in the acidity of the solution.

A pH of precisely 7 indicates that the solution is neutral, i.e. the concentrations of hydrogen and hydroxide ions are equal.

A pH of 7 to 14 indicates that there is an excess of hydroxide ions, i.e. the solution is alkaline. An increase in pH here indicates an increase in the alkalinity of the solution.

The basicity of an acid refers to the number of replaceable hydrogen atoms per molecule, thus the basicity of phosphoric acid, H_3PO_4, is 3, that of sulphuric acid, H_2SO_4, is 2 and that of hydrochloric acid, HCl, is 1. For some acids, particularly organic ones, the basicity cannot be inferred from the formula: e.g. ethanoic acid, $H_4C_2O_2$, has a basicity of 1 (which might have been predicted if the formula had been written CH_3COOH).

Indicators

The pH of a solution and the progress of a neutralization reaction may be seen by using a few drops of a universal indicator, a substance that changes its colour according to the pH of the solution.

Some common indicators, with their colours under conditions of different pH, are given in the following table:

Indicator	Acidic conditions	Neutral conditions	Alkaline conditions
litmus	red	purple	blue
phenolphthalein	colourless	colourless	red
methyl orange	red-pink	yellow	yellow
a universal indicator	red or orange	yellow-green	green or blue

Oxides

Oxides that dissolve in water to produce acidic solutions are called acidic oxides or acid anhydrides, e.g. sulphur trioxide which produces sulphuric acid. Similarly, oxides that dissolve in water to produce alkaline solutions are called basic oxides, e.g. calcium oxide which reacts with water to produce calcium hydroxide which is slightly soluble.

Some oxides, although insoluble in water, will dissolve in acids, and are thus basic oxides. Copper(II) oxide, for example, dissolves in dilute nitric acid to produce copper(II) nitrate solution, and is an example of a basic oxide.

$$CuO(s) + 2HNO_3(aq) \rightarrow Cu(NO_3)_2(aq) + H_2O(l)$$

The soluble oxides of non-metals tend to produce acidic aqueous solutions, and the oxides of many metals are basic. Oxides such as carbon monoxide that hardly dissolve in water, acids or alkalis are called neutral oxides. Other oxides which will dissolve in both acidic and alkaline solutions are called amphoteric oxides. For example, zinc oxide (acting as a base) dissolves in dilute sulphuric acid to produce zinc sulphate.

$$ZnO(s) + H_2SO_4(aq) \rightarrow ZnSO_4(aq) + H_2O(l)$$

It also (acting as an acidic oxide) dissolves in aqueous sodium hydroxide to produce sodium zincate.

$$ZnO(s) + 2NaOH(aq) + H_2O(l) \rightarrow Na_2[Zn(OH)_4](aq)$$

Peroxides are the salts of the very weak acid hydrogen peroxide (H_2O_2), and higher oxides are compounds that contain more oxygen than would be expected if the metal had its usual oxidation state. Peroxides give hydrogen peroxide when treated with dilute mineral acids, but higher oxides do not. Mixed oxides can be considered to be formed from two oxides because they react with dilute acids producing either two salts, or one salt and one oxide, e.g. dilead(II) lead(IV) oxide, Pb_3O_4, also called red lead or trilead tetraoxide.

$$Pb_3O_4(s) + 4HNO_3(aq) \rightarrow 2Pb(NO_3)_2(aq) + PbO_2(s)$$
$$+ 2H_2O(l)$$

Salts

When all of the replaceable hydrogen in an acid has been replaced by a metal, a normal salt is produced, e.g. sodium carbonate, Na_2CO_3. If, however, only part of the replaceable hydrogen has been replaced by a metal in this way, the resulting compound is called an acid salt, e.g. sodium hydrogencarbonate $NaHCO_3$.

Basic salts are compounds which contain the normal salt combined with a metal oxide or hydroxide: e.g. basic copper(II) carbonate, $CuCO_3 \cdot Cu(OH)_2$ or $Cu_2CO_3(OH)_2$, and hydrated salts are salts that contain water of crystallization in their solid structure. An example of a hydrated salt is crystalline copper(II) sulphate, $CuSO_4 \cdot 5H_2O$.

Salts take their names from the positive ion (metal or

ammonium ion) and the acid from which they are derived (negative ion or acid radical). Some common examples are given in the following table:

Acid		Radical	
Name	*Formula*	*Name*	*Formula*
carbonic	H_2CO_3	carbonate	CO_3^{2-}
		hydrogen-carbonate	HCO_3^-
ethanoic (acetic)	CH_3COOH	ethanoate (acetate)	CH_3COO^-
nitric	HNO_3	nitrate	NO_3^-
phosphoric	H_3PO_4	phosphate	PO_4^{3-}
hydrogen sulphide (hydrosulphuric)	H_2S	sulphide	S^{2-}
sulphurous	H_2SO_3	sulphite	SO_3^{2-}
sulphuric	H_2SO_4	sulphate	SO_4^{2-}
		hydrogen-sulphate	HSO_4^-
hydrochloric	HCl	chloride	Cl^-

Salts are electrically neutral, and the chemical formula of a salt represents the ions present in the proportions required to achieve electrical neutrality. Solutions of salts are not always neutral (i.e. have a pH = 7) because they often react slightly with water (hydrolysis). Although sodium chloride, sodium nitrate and sodium sulphate solutions are neutral, solutions of iron(III) chloride, copper(II) sulphate and sodium hydrogensulphate are acidic and solutions of sodium ethanoate, sodium carbonate and sodium hydrogencarbonate are alkaline.

The ending of the acid radical often indicates the quantity of oxygen present. For example,

-ide indicates no oxygen,	e.g. sulphide S^{2-}
-ite indicates some oxygen,	e.g. sulphite SO_3^{2-}
-ate indicates more oxygen,	e.g. sulphate SO_4^{2-}

The Preparation of Salts

The following are the most common ways of preparing salts. Many involve the neutralization of acids.

1. *Metal + acid*
   E.g. $Zn(s) + 2HCl(aq) \rightarrow ZnCl_2(aq) + H_2(g)$
   This is a redox reaction because the metal is oxidized, i.e. it loses electrons forming cations.

   $$Zn(s) + 2H^+(aq) \rightarrow Zn^{2+}(aq) + H_2(g)$$

2. *Insoluble base + acid*
   E.g. $CuO(s) + H_2SO_4(aq) \rightarrow CuSO_4(aq) + H_2O(l)$

3. *Alkali(soluble base) + acid*
   E.g. $2NaOH(aq) + H_2SO_4(aq) \rightarrow Na_2SO_4(aq) + 2H_2O(l)$
   This can be done by titration.

4. *Carbonate + acid*
   E.g. $CaCO_3(s) + 2HCl(aq) \rightarrow CaCl_2(aq) + H_2O(l)$
   $$+ CO_2(g)$$

   This reaction may be considered as a *displacement* reaction. Hydrochloric acid is stronger than carbonic acid, and it thus displaces it from its salt (the carbonate). The weak acid then decomposes and produces carbon dioxide gas and water.
   A similar reaction will occur between a strong acid and the salts of other weak acids.

   E.g. $FeS(s) + 2HCl(aq) \rightarrow FeCl_2(aq) + H_2S(g)$

   If a soluble carbonate is used, i.e. sodium carbonate, the reaction may be done by titration.

5. *Precipitation (ionic association)*
   This method may be used to prepare insoluble salts, e.g. in the chloride and sulphate tests.

   $$AgNO_3(aq) + HCl(aq) \rightarrow AgCl(s) + HNO_3(aq)$$
   or $\qquad Ag^+(aq) + Cl^-(aq) \rightarrow AgCl(s),$
   and $BaCl_2(aq) + H_2SO_4(aq) \rightarrow BaSO_4(s) + 2HCl(aq)$
   or $\qquad Ba^{2+}(aq) + SO_4^{2-}(aq) \rightarrow BaSO_4(s)$

6. *Direct synthesis*
   Some elements will combine directly to produce simple salts. This approach must be adopted if the salt is likely to be hydrolysed extensively.

   E.g. $Fe(s) + S(s) \rightarrow FeS(s)$

   $2Fe(s) + 3Cl_2(g) \rightarrow 2FeCl_3(s)$

   However, iron(II) chloride is produced if hydrochloric acid or hydrogen chloride is used.

   $Fe(s) + 2HCl(aq) \rightarrow FeCl_2(aq) + H_2(g)$

   $Fe(s) + 2HCl(g) \rightarrow FeCl_2(s) + H_2(g)$

   Aluminium always has a valency of three and so there is no restriction on whether chlorine or hydrogen chloride or hydrochloric acid is used to produce aluminum chloride. However, if hydrochloric acid is used, hydrated aluminium chloride is produced; this cannot be dehydrated by heating because hydrolysis occurs.

Questions

1 Element X is burned in oxygen and the product of this reaction dissolves in water giving an acidic solution. X could be

   A sulphur.
   B calcium.
   C iron.
   D copper.
   E sodium.

2 An element, Q, forms an oxide, QO_3, which dissolves in water to give an acidic solution. In which one of the following groups of the Periodic Table is Q likely to be?

   A Group I
   B Group II
   C Group IV
   D Group VI
   E Group VII

3   Which of the following compounds containing hydrogen
    is an acid in aqueous solution?

    A   hydrogen chloride
    B   methane
    C   ammonia
    D   sodium hydride
    E   calcium hydride

4   Which of the following aqueous solutions, each containing
    1 mol/dm³ of solute, will have the lowest pH?

    A   sugar
    B   sodium carbonate
    C   sulphuric acid
    D   ethanoic acid
    E   sodium hydroxide

5   Which of the following gases found in the air will cause
    rain water to be slightly acidic?

    A   nitrogen
    B   oxygen
    C   argon
    D   methane
    E   carbon dioxide

6   Which of the following numbers represents the
    approximate pH of ethanoic acid (1 mol/dm³,
    vinegar)?

    A   1
    B   4
    C   7
    D   10
    E   14

7   Which of the following pairs of dilute aqueous solutions
    when mixed together will *not* produce a precipitate?

    A   barium chloride and sodium nitrate
    B   barium nitrate and sodium sulphate
    C   silver nitrate and sodium chloride
    D   calcium nitrate and potassium carbonate
    E   iron(III) chloride and sodium hydroxide

8 Which of the following bases produces an alkaline solution when shaken with water?

   A   zinc oxide
   B   iron(III) oxide
   C   copper(II) oxide
   D   calcium oxide
   E   lead(II) oxide

9 Sodium hydrogencarbonate solution ($1 \ mol/dm^3$) has a pH of about

   A   1
   B   4
   C   7
   D   10
   E   14

10 Which of the following salts when dissolved in water produces an alkaline solution?

   A   sodium hydrogencarbonate
   B   sodium hydrogensulphate
   C   sodium sulphate
   D   sodium nitrate
   E   sodium chloride

11 Which of the following pairs of substances would react to form a salt and water only?

   A   Zinc and dilute sulphuric acid
   B   potassium carbonate and nitric acid
   C   copper and concentrated sulphuric acid
   D   iron(II) sulphide and hydrochloric acid
   E   sodium hydroxide and nitric acid

12 Which of the following chlorides is prepared by precipitation, followed by filtration and drying?

   A   silver chloride
   B   sodium chloride
   C   iron(II) chloride
   D   carbon tetrachloride
   E   phosphorus pentachloride

13 Which of the following acids has the highest basicity?

    A   sulphuric acid
    B   phosphoric acid
    C   hydrochloric acid
    D   nitric acid
    E   ethanoic acid

14 Which of the following sulphates is very soluble in water?

    A   lead(II) sulphate
    B   barium sulphate
    C   calcium sulphate
    D   magnesium sulphate
    E   iron(II) sulphate

15 Which of the following salts when dissolved in water
    produces an acidic solution?

    A   sodium chloride
    B   sodium nitrate
    C   sodium sulphate
    D   sodium hydrogensulphate
    E   sodium hydrogencarbonate

Select the appropriate response from the following properties
of sulphuric acid for *questions 16–20*.

    A   forms an acid salt
    B   forms a normal salt
    C   forms an insoluble salt
    D   acts as a dehydrating agent
    E   acts as a non-volatile agent

Which of these responses *best* describes

16 concentrated sulphuric acid reacting with solid sodium
    chloride?

17 making sodium hydrogensulphate from dilute sulphuric
    acid and sodium hydroxide solution?

18 sulphuric acid reacting with calcium chloride solution?

19 obtaining carbon from sugar?

20 making hydrated sodium sulphate crystals?

Select the appropriate response from the following list of types of oxide for *questions 21—25*.

A   acidic
B   basic
C   amphoteric
D   neutral
E   higher

Which of these responses *best* describes

21   carbon monoxide?

22   zinc oxide?

23   calcium oxide?

24   carbon dioxide?

25   sulphur trioxide?

Select the appropriate response from the following list of methods of preparing salts for *questions 26—30*.

A   metal with acid gives salt and hydrogen
B   insoluble metal oxide with acid gives salt and water
C   soluble metal hydroxide with acid gives salt and water
D   mixing two soluble salts gives an insoluble salt and a solution
E   direct synthesis using two elements

Which of these responses best describes the preparation of

26   barium sulphate from barium nitrate solution and sodium sulphate solution?

27   hydrated iron(II) sulphate crystals from iron and dilute sulphuric acid?

28   hydrated copper(II) sulphate from copper(II) oxide and dilute sulphuric acid?

29   anhydrous iron(III) chloride from iron and chlorine?

30   sodium nitrate by the titration of sodium hydroxide solution with dilute nitric acid?

7 The Mole Concept

Atomic, Molecular and Molar Masses

The *relative atomic mass* (A_r) of an element is the average (weighted mean) mass of its atoms, compared to the mass of an atom of carbon (the nuclide $^{12}_6C$) taken as precisely 12.

The *relative molecular mass* (M_r) of an element or compound is defined in the same way, but it is usually calculated by adding together the relative atomic masses in the proportions indicated by the formula.

The *molar mass* (M) of a species (element, compound, ion, etc.) is the mass of a mole of that species. The Avogadro constant is 6.0×10^{23} mole^{-1} (species per mole) and is the number of carbon atoms in 12 g of the nuclide $^{12}_6C$. Thus the molar mass of an element or a compound is its relative molecular mass considered in grams. Counting in units of 6.0×10^{23} is the chemist's way of dealing with the huge numbers of atoms or molecules present even in small samples of substances. To count in small numbers such as pairs, tens, dozens etc. would not reduce the problem significantly, and so the chemist counts in moles.

Formulae

If water is analysed it is found that it consists of 11.1 % by mass of hydrogen and 88.9 % by mass of oxygen. The relative atomic masses of hydrogen and oxygen are 1 and 16 respectively, i.e. the molar masses of their atoms are 1 g and 16 g. Consider 100 g of water:

$$\text{Amount of hydrogen} = \frac{11.1}{1} = 11.1 \text{ moles of atoms}$$

$$\text{Amount of oxygen} = \frac{88.9}{16} = 5.55 \text{ moles of atoms}$$

The amounts of hydrogen and oxygen, in terms of moles of atoms, are in the ratio of 11.1 to 5.55, i.e. $2:1$. Thus the empirical formula (simplest formula) of water, which indicates the ratio of the numbers of atoms, is H_2O. Notice that the

subscript 1 is not written after the O for oxygen because
writing the symbol implies the presence of one atom in the
molecule.

The true or molecular formula of water may be H_2O or
some multiple of this, such as H_4O_2, etc. One way of deciding
the value of the multiple is to measure the density of a
substance in the gaseous state. The relative, or vapour density
of a gas is its density compared to that of hydrogen under the
same conditions of temperature and pressure. It can be proved
that for a gas

$$\text{relative molecular mass} = 2 \times \text{relative density}$$

For a solid or liquid that cannot be vaporized, the method of
finding the multiple is more difficult.

If ethene is analysed it is found to contain 86% by mass of
carbon and 14% by mass of hydrogen. (You should be able to
prove that its empirical formula is CH_2.) The relative density
of ethene is 14, so its relative molecular mass is 28. The
relative molecular mass corresponding to the empirical
formula is 14, so CH_2 cannot be the molecular formula. If the
empirical formula is doubled, the corresponding relative
molecular mass is 28, which is correct. The molecular formula
of ethene is therefore C_2H_4.

Percentage Composition

Using relative molecular masses also gives us a method of
finding the percentage composition of substances. For example,
the relative molecular mass of hydrogen sulphide (H_2S) is
$(1 \times 2) + 32 = 34$. Of this 2/34 is hydrogen and 32/34 is
sulphur. Thus.

$$\text{Percentage of hydrogen} = \frac{2}{34} \times 100 = 5.9$$

$$\text{Percentage of sulphur} = \frac{32}{34} \times 100 = 94.1$$

When doing calculations like this, check that the sum of the
percentages is 100.

Many crystalline substances contain some water of
crystallization, which means that some water is loosely attached
to the compound. These are known as hydrated salts and in
some cases the water can be driven off by gentle heating. For

example, Epsom salts (hydrated magnesium sulphate) can be shown to contain 51.2% of water by mass.

$$M_r(MgSO_4) = 24 + 32 + (16 \times 4) = 120$$
$$M_r(H_2O) = (1 \times 2) + 16 = 18$$

Consider 100 g of the hydrated salt

Amount of magnesium sulphate $(MgSO_4) = \dfrac{48.8}{120} = 0.41$ moles

Amount of water $(H_2O) = \dfrac{51.2}{18} = 2.84$ moles

The amounts of magnesium sulphate and water, in terms of moles, are in the ratio of 0.41 to 2.84, or 1 : 7 (within the limits of experimental error). Thus the formula of Epsom salts is $MgSO_4 \cdot 7H_2O$.

Equations

When we write an *equation* to represent a chemical reaction we are simplifying matters to the molecular (atomic) level, e.g.,

$$CuO + H_2 \rightarrow Cu + H_2O$$

In an experiment we may be dealing with 6.0×10^{23} particles of each species, i.e. one mole of each, so we can write the reacting quantities under the formulae in the equation thus:

$$CuO + H_2 \rightarrow Cu + H_2O$$
$$80\,g \quad 2\,g \quad 64\,g \quad 18\,g$$

This experiment could be carried out using some multiple or sub-multiple of the molar mass. For example, if one-tenth of a mole of copper oxide (8 g) reacted in this way, one-tenth of a mole of copper (6.4 g) would be produced. In calculations it is not necessary to calculate the quantities of substances which are stated to be sufficient or in excess, or are not directly needed in the question.

Consider another reaction, when magnesium sulphate reacts with sodium hydroxide in aqueous solution to produce a precipitate of magnesium hydroxide.

$$MgSO_4(aq) + 2NaOH(aq) \rightarrow Mg(OH)_2(s) + Na_2SO_4(aq)$$

If the precipitate is filtered off and heated, magnesium oxide is produced.

$$Mg(OH)_2(s) \rightarrow MgO(s) + H_2O(l)$$

By using these balanced chemical equations, if we started with, say, 12 g magnesium sulphate, we could calculate the mass of magnesium oxide that would be produced.

$$MgSO_4 \rightarrow Mg(OH)_2 \rightarrow MgO$$

120 g   40 g

Hence,

$$12 \text{ g } MgSO_4 \rightarrow 4 \text{ g } MgO$$

If the experiment starts with a hydrated salt, then the water of crystallization must be part of the calculation, e.g.

$$MgSO_4 \cdot 7H_2O \rightarrow Mg(OH)_2 \rightarrow MgO$$

246 g   40 g

Where gases are concerned, it is often convenient to measure volumes. The volume of a mole of gas under the standard conditions of temperature ($0°C$) and pressure (101.3 kPa) is 22.4 dm³ (litres), and this quantity can be used in calculations instead of mass. Note that some examination boards consider the molar volume to be 24 dm³ at room temperature and pressure (a vague statement). Carefully check the rubric of your examination paper therefore, before you use this quantity rather than 22.4 dm³.

Consider for example the catalytic decomposition of hydrogen peroxide, for which the catalyst is often manganese(IV) oxide.

$$2H_2O_2(aq) \rightarrow 2H_2O(l) + O_2(g)$$

Considering moles of these substances:

2 × 34 g   2 × 18 g   32 g   or   22.4 dm³

If, in an experiment, we start with 1 dm³ of a solution of hydrogen peroxide containing 30 g/dm³, then:

$$2H_2O_2 \rightarrow O_2$$

By equation: 68 g   22.4 dm³

In experiment: 30 g $\dfrac{30 \times 22.4}{68}$

$$= 10 \text{ dm}^3$$

Thus 1 dm³ of the hydrogen peroxide solution gives 10 dm³ of oxygen. Such a solution is described as 10-volume hydrogen peroxide, and this may be sold for use as an antiseptic or for bleaching hair. (It should be diluted to about 1 volume before use.)

Concentration

Many solutions used in laboratories are described in terms of their molar concentrations. Dilute sulphuric acid, for example, may be used as a 1 mol/dm³ solution (1 M). The relative molecular mass of sulphuric acid, H_2SO_4, is 98, so the dilute acid contains 98 g/dm³ of sulphuric acid, i.e. it is almost 90 % water. (Now prove in the same way that dilute hydrochloric acid, if 1 mol/dm³, is over 96 % water.)

If the concentration of one solution is known, the concentration of another solution with which it reacts may be found by titration. For example, sodium hydroxide solution can be titrated with dilute hydrochloric acid, using litmus or some other indicator which will show by a change in colour when the end-point or neutral point of the reaction has been reached. The equation for the reaction is

$$NaOH + HCl \rightarrow NaCl + H_2O$$

In v cm³ of a solution which contains c mol/dm³ of solute there are $vc/1000$ moles of solute. From the equation we can see that one mole of alkali (sodium hydroxide solution) reacts with one mole of hydrochloric acid, so when the neutral point is reached:

$vc/1000$ moles of alkali react with $vc/1000$ moles of acid.

In general terms, for the reaction in which a molecules of A react with b molecules of B to give d molecules of D and e molecules of E:

$$aA + bB \rightarrow dD + eE$$

$$\frac{v_A \times c_A}{v_B \times c_B} = \frac{a}{b}$$

$$[1 \text{ dm}^3 = 1 \text{ litre (symbol l or L) and}$$
$$1 \text{ dm}^3 = 1000 \text{ cm}^3 \text{ (ml or mL).}]$$

Questions

The relative atomic masses for questions in this chapter are to be found on page 124.

1 Burning magnesium close to a vessel containing hydrogen and chlorine causes a reaction represented by the following equation

$$H_2(g) + Cl_2(g) \rightarrow 2HCl(g)$$

Hence it can be deduced that

A hydrogen chloride is monatomic.
B atoms of hydrogen chloride are obtained.
C the volume of the products is twice that of the reactants (all measured at s.t.p.).
D there is a contraction in gas volume as the reaction proceeds.
E the volume of the reactants is the same as that of the product (all measured at s.t.p.).

2 Which of the following is the empirical formula of an organic compound containing 40% of carbon, 6.7% of hydrogen and 53.3% of oxygen, by mass.

A CH_2O

B CH_4O

C C_2H_4O

D C_2H_6O

E $C_2H_4O_2$

3 The synthesis of ammonia is represented by the following equation.

$$N_2(g) + 3H_2(g) \rightarrow 2NH_3(g)$$

When 100 cm³ of nitrogen react, the volumes of the other gases are

A 100 cm³ of hydrogen and 100 cm³ of ammonia.
B 100 cm³ of hydrogen and 200 cm³ of ammonia.
C 200 cm³ of hydrogen and 300 cm³ of ammonia.
D 300 cm³ of hydrogen and 200 cm³ of ammonia.
E 300 cm³ of hydrogen and 400 cm³ of ammonia.

4 Which of the following solutions does *not* contain enough sodium hydroxide to precipitate all the copper(II) ions present in $50 \, cm^3$ of $1 \, mol/dm^3$ copper(II) sulphate solution?

$$Cu^{2+}(aq) + 2OH^-(aq) \rightarrow Cu(OH)_2(s)$$

A $100 \, cm^3$ of $1 \, mol/dm^3$ NaOH
B $75 \, cm^3$ of $2 \, mol/dm^3$ NaOH
C $50 \, cm^3$ of $2 \, mol/dm^3$ NaOH
D $30 \, cm^3$ of $3 \, mol/dm^3$ NaOH
E $25 \, cm^3$ of $4 \, mol/dm^3$ NaOH

5 The gaseous hydrocarbon ethene burns in oxygen to give carbon dioxide and water according to the following equation.

$$C_2H_4(g) + 3O_2(g) \rightarrow 2CO_2(g) + 2H_2O(l)$$

What is the volume of the resulting gas, in cm^3 at room temperature, when $10 \, cm^3$ of ethene is sparked with $50 \, cm^3$ of oxygen?

A 20
B 30
C 40
D 50
E 60

6 Zinc dissolves in hot sodium hydroxide solution according to the following equation.

$$Zn(s) + 2NaOH(aq) + 2H_2O(l) \rightarrow Na_2Zn(OH)_4(aq) + H_2(g)$$

On this evidence it may be concluded that

A $65 \, g$ of zinc will dissolve in $2 \, dm^3$ of $1 \, mol/dm^3$ sodium hydroxide.
B zinc is amphoteric.
C 1 mole of zinc will release $44.8 \, dm^3$ of hydrogen.
D $65 \, g$ of zinc will give $1 \, g$ of hydrogen.
E zinc is a transition element.

7 The number of atoms in 2 g of helium is
A 1.5×10^{23}
B 3.0×10^{23}
C 4.0×10^{23}
D 6.0×10^{23}
E 12.0×10^{23}

8 Boron forms a gaseous hydride, diborane, which has an atomicity of 8. On analysis, 2.8 g of diborane were found to contain 0.6 g of hydrogen.
Therefore the formula of diborane is

A BH_3
B BH_7
C B_2H_6
D B_3H
E B_6H_2

9 What volume, in cm^3, of 0.1 mol/dm^3 hydrochloric acid will neutralize 20 cm^3 of 0.125 mol/dm^3 sodium hydroxide solution?

A 10
B 16
C 20
D 25
E 30

10 Hydrogen peroxide in aqueous solution decomposes on warming to give oxygen.

$$2H_2O_2(aq) \rightarrow 2H_2O(l) + O_2(g)$$

If 100 cm^3 of an x mol/dm^3 solution of hydrogen peroxide yields 2.8 dm^3 of oxygen, under standard conditions of temperature and pressure, the value of x is

A 0.1.
B 0.25.
C 0.5.
D 1.0.
E 2.5.

11   Sodium hydroxide solution and dilute sulphuric acid react
     according to the following equation.

$$2NaOH + H_2SO_4 \rightarrow Na_2SO_4 + 2H_2O$$

What volume (in cm^3) of $0.5\,mol/dm^3$ sulphuric acid will
neutralize $25\,cm^3$ of $0.2\,mol/dm^3$ sodium hydroxide
solution

A   5
B   20
C   25
D   31.25
E   500

12   What amount in moles of sulphate ions is there in
     $250\,cm^3$ of a $0.1\,mol/dm^3$ solution of sodium sulphate?

A   0.025
B   0.1
C   25
D   250
E   4

13   Silver forms an insoluble chromate. $10\,cm^3$ of a solution
     of a soluble chromate require $20\,cm^3$ of a solution of
     silver nitrate $(AgNO_3)$ of the same concentration (in
     mol/dm^3) to precipitate all of the chromate ions. What is
     the charge on the chromate ion?

A   −1
B   −2
C   0
D   +1
E   +2

14   During the electrolysis of fused lead(II) bromide, $5.175\,g$
     of lead were deposited on the cathode. What mass (in
     grams) of bromine would have been liberated at the
     anode during this experiment?

A   2
B   4
C   8
D   16
E   160

15   Iodine and sodium thiosulphate react together to give sodium iodide and sodium tetrathionate.

$$I_2(s) + 2Na_2S_2O_3(aq) \rightarrow 2NaI(aq) + Na_2S_4O_6(aq)$$

Which of the following statements is *not* true?

A   Iodine is an oxidizing agent

B   1 mole of iodine will react with 2 moles of sodium thiosulphate.

C   A colour change from brown to colourless occurs during the reaction.

D   The sodium tetrathionate is the oxidizing agent.

E   At the end point of the reaction starch indicator will go from blue-black to colourless.

Select the appropriate response from the following for *questions 16–20*

    A   0
    B   1
    C   2
    D   3
    E   4

16   How many hydrogen atoms are contained in the empirical formula of a compound containing 75 % carbon and 25 % hydrogen by mass?

17   How many oxygen atoms are contained in the empirical formula of an oxide of iron containing 70 % iron by mass?

18   What is the atomicity of xenon, if 131 g of this gas occupies 22.4 dm^3 under standard conditions of temperature and pressure?

19   How many atoms of chlorine are contained in the empirical formula of the anhydrous chloride of tin, 2.61 g of which contains 1.19 g of tin?

20   If 1.4 g of iron reacts exactly with 0.8 g of sulphur, how many atoms of iron are found in the empirical formula of this sulphide?

Use the following list of gas volumes (in cm³) to select responses for *questions 21—25*. These questions refer to the complete combustion of a 10 cm³ sample of butane, C_4H_{10}, according to the following equation.

$$2C_4H_{10} + 13O_2 \rightarrow 8CO_2 + 10H_2O$$

A   15
B   35
C   40
D   65
E   80

Which of these responses describes the volume

21   of oxygen required for complete combustion?

22   of carbon dioxide produced in the experiment?

23   of carbon dioxide produced if 330 cm³ of air (20 % oxygen) were used in the experiment?

24   contraction if the experiment is performed at room temperature?

25   expansion if the experiment is performed at above 100 °C?

8 Energy Changes and Rates of Reaction

Endothermic and Exothermic Reactions

Energy is often released when chemical reactions take place. Such reactions are said to be exothermic. The energy change (ΔH) is negative since the energy level of the reacting substances (the reactants) is higher than that of the products of the reaction.

When the energy level of the products of a reaction is above that of the reactants, the reaction is said to be endothermic, and ΔH is positive. Whether the reaction is exothermic or endothermic, its rate may be governed by its activation energy (see Chapter 9). The energy change of a reaction studied under constant pressure is called its enthalpy change.

Combustion

When some substances burn, the oxidation reaction sometimes occurs only at its surface. Heat and sometimes light or sound may be emitted. Some fuels are solids like coke, wood or paper; some are liquids like petrol, paraffin or methylated spirits; and others are gases like methane, propane or butane. The oxidizing agent is not always oxygen. Dutch metal (an alloy of copper and zinc) in powder form burns spontaneously in an atmosphere of chlorine, producing a mixture of copper(II) chloride and zinc chloride.

The energy change in reactions is quoted in kilojoules per mole of equation (kJ/mol). Some typical examples of combustions are:

$$C(s) + O_2(g) \rightarrow CO_2(g); \qquad\qquad \Delta H = -394\,kJ/mol$$
$$CH_4(g) + 2O_2(g) \rightarrow CO_2(g) + 2H_2O(l); \quad \Delta H = -890\ kJ/mol$$
$$2H_2(g) + O_2(g) \rightarrow 2H_2O(l); \qquad\qquad \Delta H = -572\ kJ/mol$$
$$C_2H_5OH(l) + 3O_2(g) \rightarrow 2CO_2(g) + 3H_2O(l);$$
$$\Delta H = -1371\ kJ/mol$$

Solutions

When solutes dissolve in solvents there is an energy change, and thus substances will have different solubilities at different temperatures. For most substances the solubility increases with increase in temperature because dissolution is an endothermic process. Some typical examples of solutes dissolving in water are:

$NaCl(s) \rightarrow NaCl(aq);$ $\quad\quad\quad\quad\quad \Delta H = +4$ kJ/mol

$NaNO_3(s) \rightarrow NaNO_3(aq);$ $\quad\quad\quad \Delta H = +20$ kJ/mol

$NH_4Cl(s) \rightarrow NH_4Cl(aq);$ $\quad\quad\quad \Delta H = +15$ kJ/mol

$Ca(OH)_2(s) \rightarrow Ca(OH)_2(aq);$ $\quad\quad \Delta H = -16$ kJ/mol

Neutralization

There is an energy change when an acid is neutralized by a base. When a strong acid (e.g. the mineral acid, hydrochloric acid) is neutralized by a strong base (e.g. sodium hydroxide), the enthalpy change is always -57 kJ/mol. Hydrochloric acid and sodium hydroxide contain ions and the molecular reaction in aqueous solution.

$$NaOH + HCl \rightarrow NaCl + H_2O$$

is better written to emphasize this as

$$Na^+ + OH^- + H^+ + Cl^- \rightarrow Na^+ + Cl^- + H_2O$$

The sodium and chloride ions are 'spectators' and so, in simple terms, the reaction may be expressed as

$$OH^-(aq) + H^+(aq) \rightarrow H_2O(l)$$

This equation describes the reaction between any strong acid and strong base.

Fuels

Most of our energy for industrial and domestic use comes from fossil fuels. Millions of years ago coal, oil and natural gas (methane) were formed and trapped under the surface of the earth. Today we are using these resources faster than we are finding new supplies but at current prices it is sometimes uneconomic to extract all that we do find. Oil production reached a peak in the 1970s and its use may decline for the remainder of the twentieth century. Natural gas, like oil, may be scarce and expensive in the second half of the twenty-first century, whereas coal may be reasonably plentiful for several centuries.

Natural fuels will not last for ever, and hence there is a search for alternative sources of energy. The sun, wind and tides are all possibilities. Over two-thirds of our electricity is generated using coal as the boiler fuel. The supply of uranium, as employed in Magnox reactors, like fossil fuels, will be exhausted if its use continues at its present rate.

Cells

In a Daniell cell, a chemical reaction produces energy in the form of an electric current. The overall reaction is

$$Zn(s) + CuSO_4(aq) \rightarrow Cu(s) + ZnSO_4(aq)$$

In a dry cell the zinc atoms become zinc ions as the cell supplies a current. Both of these cells are primary cells and cannot be recharged after use. The lead accumulator, used as a car battery, is a secondary cell because it can be recharged after use. In a fuel cell, hydrogen and oxygen combine to form water. However, the reagents for all of these cells have to be manufactured first, and more energy is used up in making them than they will give when they are used.

The Effect of Heating Substances

There are several types of reaction that can occur when a substance (whether molecular or ionic) is heated.

1. A physical reaction which may be
   (a) a solid changing into a liquid
   (b) a liquid changing into a gas
   (c) a solid changing into a gas (volatilization)
   (d) a solid changing its structure.

When elements such as iron and sulphur change their structure on heating, this is one type of allotropy. For compounds such as ammonium nitrate this is called polymorphism.

Physical reactions are reversible.

2. A chemical reaction may occur with air, unless the substance is heated in a vacuum. For example,

$$2Mg(s) + O_2(g) \rightarrow 2MgO(s)$$

3. One type of chemical reaction that may occur is thermal decomposition. In this case a substance splits up into simpler substances that do not recombine on cooling together. For example,

$$2Pb(NO_3)_2(s) \rightarrow 2PbO(s) + 4NO_2(g) + O_2(g)$$

4. When a substance splits up into simpler substances which will recombine on cooling together, this is called thermal dissociation. For example,

$$NH_4Cl(s) \rightleftharpoons NH_3(g) + HCl(g)$$

and $\quad CaCO_3(s) \rightleftharpoons CaO(s) + CO_2(g)$

The Effect of the State of the Reactants upon Reaction Rate

1. The state of division of a solid. A powdered solid has a higher surface area than the same mass of solid in the form of large lumps. The powder therefore will react faster, as can be seen if powdered calcium carbonate and marble chips react separately with moderately concentrated hydrochloric acid, and the volumes of carbon dioxide produced at various times are measured.

$$CaCO_3(s) + 2HCl(aq) \rightarrow CaCl_2(aq) + H_2O(l) + CO_2(g)$$

2. The concentration of a solute in a solution. In some cases the rate depends directly on the concentration but in other cases there is not a linear relationship. For example, when sodium thiosulphate is acidified, sulphur is precipitated. The reaction rate depends directly on the concentration of the sodium thiosulphate, but the relationship between the rate and the concentration of the acid is complex.

$$Na_2S_2O_3(aq) + 2HCl(aq) \rightarrow 2NaCl(aq) + H_2O(l) + SO_2(aq) + S(s)$$

3. The pressure of a gas. The precise relationship between rate and pressure must be determined by experiment.

The Supply of Energy

Generally, the energy involved in chemical reactions is heat, but it could be in some other form such as light or mechanical energy.

When the reagents in a chemical reaction are heated, the reaction proceeds faster. The energy supplied activates some molecules which react and they, in turn, activate others. Some reactions such as the neutralization of an acid by an alkali have a negligible activation energy at room temperature. Other reactions such as the syntheses of water, ammonia and hydrogen chloride have fairly large activation energies.

The effect of temperature on the rate of a reaction can be shown by putting zinc or magnesium (or alternatively calcium carbonate or sodium thiosulphate) into hydrochloric acid at various temperatures.

$$Mg(s) + 2HCl(aq) \rightarrow MgCl_2(aq) + H_2(g)$$
$$Zn(s) + 2HCl(aq) \rightarrow ZnCl_2(aq) + H_2(g)$$

If such reactions are conducted at different temperatures, it will be seen that hydrogen etc. is produced at a faster rate at higher temperatures.

In photography, light falls on the film which contains silver bromide and causes it to decompose.

$$2AgBr(s) \rightarrow 2Ag(s) + Br_2(l)$$

The bromine then reacts with other materials in the film.

A cap being fired in a toy gun is an example of mechanical energy supplying the activation energy, as is the striking of a match.

Catalysts

These are substances which increase the rate of a chemical reaction. They can be recovered at the end of the reaction, unchanged in mass but possibly changed in physical form. A catalyst in lump form, for example, may be recovered at the end of the reaction as a powder. (Substances which decrease the rate of a reaction are called inhibitors.)

Catalysts increase the rate of reactions by reducing the activation energy, and thus making alternative reaction pathways possible. Different catalysts may be used for the same reaction. For example the catalytic decomposition of hydrogen peroxide is usually carried out in the laboratory using manganese(IV) oxide, but there are enzymes in the blood which are just as effective, and ensure that we are not poisoned by any accumulation of peroxides in our bodies.

$$2H_2O_2(aq) \rightarrow 2H_2O(l) + O_2(g)$$

The hydrolysis (reaction with water) of starches yielding sugars is also catalysed by enzymes and by dilute acids. Enzymes are very specific catalysts found associated with living cells but able to act away from them. The enzymes in yeast, for example, catalyse the fermentation of starches and sugars to give ethanol.

By amylase: starch → maltose   ⎫   Both stages catalysed

By maltase: maltose → glucose   ⎬   by dilute acids

By sucrase
or acid: sucrose → glucose   +   fructose
('sugar')

By a zymase
complex: glucose → ethanol   +   carbon dioxide
(or fructose)

Reversible Reactions

The influence of the state of the reagents, supply of energy and catalysts on the rate of a reversible reaction is more complex than in the case of a one-way reaction. Many industrial processes involve reversible reactions. Typical examples of such processes are the steam reforming of methane, the synthesis of ammonia and the production of sulphur trioxide. If the reaction, left to right, is exothermic, then increasing the temperature will increase the rate but it will decrease the yield of the product. A catalyst does not affect the yield in a reversible reaction.

Questions

1 A catalyst always

    A slows down a chain reaction.
    B starts a reaction which would otherwise not occur at all.
    C changes the quantities of the products formed.
    D increases the activation energy of a reaction.
    E causes an increase in the rate of a reaction.

2 Which of the following equations represents an endothermic reaction?

    A $CO_2 + H_2O \rightarrow CH_2O + O_2$
    B $C + O_2 \rightarrow CO_2$
    C $2H_2 + O_2 \rightarrow 2H_2O$
    D $CH_4 + 2O_2 \rightarrow CO_2 + 2H_2O$
    E $2C_8H_{18} + 25O_2 \rightarrow 16CO_2 + 18H_2O$

3 Which of the following represents a secondary cell?

    A $Zn(s)|H_2SO_4(aq) \mathbin{\vdots\vdots} CuSO_4(aq)|Cu$

    B $Zn(s)|NH_4Cl(aq)|MnO_2(s)$

    C $Pb(s)|H_2SO_4(aq)|PbO_2(s)$

    D $Cd(s)|KOH(aq)|Ni(s)$

    E $Zn(s)|KOH(aq)|HgO(s)$

4 For the reaction represented by the equation
$H_2(g) + Cl_2(g) \rightarrow 2HCl(g); \ \Delta H = -184 \text{ kJ/mol}$
the energy change in kJ (mol of hydrogen chloride)$^{-1}$ formed is

    A -184
    B -92
    C -368
    D $+92$
    E $+184$

5 Which of the following is the *most* important factor if the rate of a reaction is to be high?

   A a large endothermic change
   B a small activation energy
   C a large activation energy
   D a small endothermic change
   E a large exothermic change

6 Which industrial process, represented by the following equations, does *not* require a catalyst?

   A $N_2 + 3H_2 \rightarrow 2NH_3$
   B $2SO_2 + O_2 \rightarrow 2SO_3$
   C $4NH_3 + 5O_2 \rightarrow 4NO + 6H_2O$
   D $H_2 + Cl_2 \rightarrow 2HCl$
   E $CH_4 + H_2O \rightarrow CO + 3H_2$

7 Which of the following fuels is usually contaminated with a significant proportion of sulphur compounds?

   A paraffin
   B wood
   C petroleum
   D North sea gas
   E natural gas

8 In a reaction between magnesium and a large excess of dilute hydrochloric acid, the hydrogen evolved was collected and measured at room temperature and pressure. If the reaction had been carried out with the same quantities of reactants, but at a higher temperature, which of the following sets of results would have been expected?

	Volume of hydrogen	Rate of hydrogen production
A	same	same
B	same	faster
C	greater	slower
D	greater	same
E	greater	faster

9 For the reaction represented by the equation

$$N_2(g) + 3H_2(g) \rightarrow 2NH_3(g); \ \Delta H = -92 \text{ kJ/mol}$$

the energy change is

A   endothermic to the extent of 46 kJ per mole of ammonia.

B   endothermic to the extent of 92 kJ per mole of ammonia.

C   exothermic to the extent of 46 kJ per mole of hydrogen.

D   exothermic to the extent of 46 kJ per mole of ammonia.

E   exothermic to the extent of 92 kJ per mole of ammonia.

10 Catalysts are often used in manufacturing processes because they

A   are cheap.

B   increase the total amount of product formed.

C   increase the amount of product formed in a given time.

D   purify the product.

E   prevent side-reactions.

11 Which of the following reactions would be expected to be the most exothermic?

A $P_4(s) + 5O_2(g) \rightarrow 2P_2O_5(s)$

B $C_{12}H_{22}O_{11}(s) + 12O_2(g) \rightarrow 12CO_2(g) + 11H_2O(l)$

C $4H(g) \rightarrow {}^4_2He(g)$

D $2O_3(g) \rightarrow 3O_2(g)$

E $4Al(s) + 3O_2(g) \rightarrow 2Al_2O_3(s)$

12 Which of the following nitrates is dangerously explosive when heated?

A   ammonium nitrate

B   sodium nitrate

C   copper(II) nitrate

D   lead(II) nitrate

E   calcium nitrate

13 The energy released per mole when various liquids are burnt completely in air are indicated in the following table

Formula	ΔH (kJ/mol)
C_2H_5OH	-1371
CH_3OH	-715
C_6H_6	-3273
$C_6H_5CH_3$	-3909
CS_2	-1076

If 1 g of each of these liquids is completely burnt, and the energy is completely absorbed by 100 g of water at 20°C, which of the following chemicals, represented by their formulae, will cause the temperature of the water to undergo the largest rise?

A C_2H_5OH
B CH_3OH
C C_6H_6
D $C_6H_5CH_3$
E CS_2

14 Which of the following processes requires a catalyst for it to proceed at a reasonable rate?

A the combustion of carbon
B the saponification of an ester
C the decomposition of hydrogen peroxide
D the synthesis of iron(II) sulphide
E the efflorescence of washing soda

15 What catalyst is used in the manufacture of sulphur trioxide from sulphur dioxide?

A manganese(IV) oxide
B nickel
C iron
D vanadium(V) oxide
E magnesium chloride

Select the appropriate response from the following curves for *questions 16–20*. The value of *y* measures the mass or volume or activity or rate and the value of *x* measures the time or temperature.

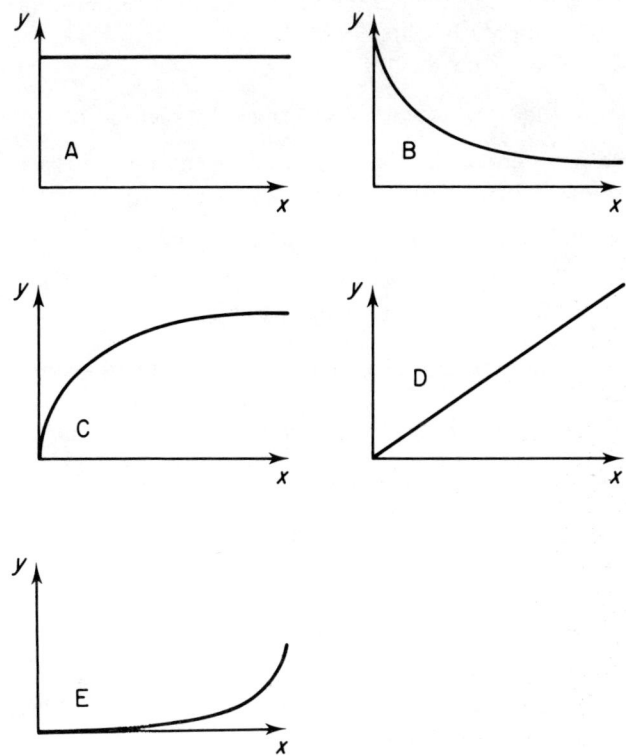

Which of these responses *best* describes

16 the mass of a corked flask containing phosphorus burning in air?

17 the activity of a sample of radioactive iodine?

18 the volume of oxygen produced during the catalytic decomposition of hydrogen peroxide?

19 the variation of the rate of a reaction with temperature?

20 the mass of a beaker containing marble chips reacting with dilute hydrochloric acid?

Select the appropriate response from the following for *questions 21—25.*

A   using the same mass but larger lumps of the solid
B   increasing the pressure of the gases
C   increasing the concentrations of the solutions
D   shining a brighter light
E   there is no way of affecting the rate of the reaction

Which of these responses *best* describes the method of

21   slowing down the reaction between marble chips and hydrochloric acid?

22   increasing the rate of conversion of silver bromide into silver?

23   increasing the rate of synthesis of ammonia?

24   increasing the rate of making barium sulphate from aqueous sodium sulphate and aqueous barium chloride?

25   increasing the radioactivity of a piece of uranium?

9 Air, Water and the Environment

The Composition of the Atmosphere

Air is a *mixture* containing nitrogen (about $\frac{4}{5}$) and oxygen about $\frac{1}{5}$), the noble gases (about 1 %), carbon dioxide (0.03 %) and water vapour (variable). It may also contain small proportions of pollutants such as smoke and sulphur dioxide.

Carbon dioxide may be removed from the air by passing it through soda-lime (a mixture of sodium hydroxide and calcium hydroxide) and oxygen may be removed by combination with an element such as magnesium which produces a solid oxide. The nitrogen left (with the noble gases) may be collected over water. It is also possible to liquefy air, and to recover the separate gases by fractional distillation of the liquid.

The Action of Heat on Substances

When elements are heated in an inert atmosphere or in a vacuum, the forces between the atoms are overcome and a. change in structure or change of phase occurs. For example, solid yellow sulphur on heating undergoes a number of colour changes due to changes in structure, resulting eventually in the formation of a dark red liquid.

The part of the air which is most reactive is oxygen, and when heated in air, those elements that have an affinity for oxygen will burn to form oxides. For example, magnesium when heated in air forms magnesium oxide, while liquid sulphur burns to form sulphur dioxide. Highly reactive metals such as magnesium may also react with the nitrogen in the air to form metal nitrides.

When compounds are heated in an inert atmosphere, only a change of phase may occur if the constituent particles have a strong affinity for each other. For example, solid lead(II) bromide on heating becomes liquid lead(II) bromide. The ease with which such a change in phase occurs gives an indication of the type of bonding in the compound.

If the affinity of the atoms in a compound is weak, thermal

decomposition may occur. For example, mercury(II) oxide on strong heating splits up and produces mercury and oxygen.

If a compound will burn in air, it may produce a mixture of the oxides of the elements contained in the compound. For example, hydrocarbons burn to form water and carbon dioxide. If the quantity of oxygen available for such a reaction is insufficient for complete combustion carbon monoxide may be produced or the flame may be smoky (due to the presence of unburnt carbon particles).

$$CH_4(g) + 2O_2(g) \rightarrow CO_2(g) + 2H_2O(l)$$
$$2CH_4(g) + 3O_2(g) \rightarrow 2CO(g) + 4H_2O(l)$$
$$CH_4(g) + O_2(g) \rightarrow C(s) + 2H_2O(l)$$

If, on heating a substance changes chemically but changes back to the original substance on cooling then, it is said to have undergone a reversible change. For example, zinc oxide is yellow when hot (above 250 °C) but white when cold. When a new chemical substance is produced on heating and cooling, the change is said to be irreversible, e.g. the thermal decomposition of lead(II) nitrate which produces lead(II) oxide, nitrogen dioxide and oxygen.

The Composition of Water

Water is the commonest and most important compound on earth. When hydrogen is burnt in air or oxygen, water is produced, indicating that it is an oxide of hydrogen. The electrolysis of dilute sulphuric acid between platinum electrodes produces two volumes of hydrogen at the cathode for every one volume of oxygen at the anode, demonstrating that the formula of water is H_2O. Water contains covalent molecules, and due to the presence of weak bonds (hydrogen bonds) between the molecules, it is a liquid at room temperature rather than a gas.

Chemical Reactions of Water

Metals that are more reactive than hydrogen, will displace hydrogen from water. For example,

$$2Na(s) + 2H_2O(l) \rightarrow 2NaOH(aq) + H_2(g)$$

In general, the more affinity a metal has for oxygen, the more vigorous this reaction will be. Potassium, for example, reacts more violently with water than does sodium, because its valency electron is further away from the nucleus of the atom and therefore held less strongly.

Steam reacts with white-hot coke to produce a mixture of carbon monoxide and hydrogen (water gas).

$$C(s) + H_2O(g) \rightarrow CO(g) + H_2(g)$$

Water combines with anhydrous salts to form hydrated salts. The formation of blue copper(II) sulphate crystals when a liquid is added to white anhydrous copper(II) sulphate indicates that the liquid contains water.

$$CuSO_4 + 5H_2O \rightarrow CuSO_4 \cdot 5H_2O$$

In hydrated salts the salt and water combine loosely but in fixed proportions (the change may be reversed by heating).

Solubility

Basic oxides dissolve in water to produce alkaline solutions, while acidic oxides will form acidic solutions.

Water is a polar solvent and will dissolve ionic compounds. The extent to which this occurs depends on the solubility of the solute, and this usually increases as the temperature increases. At constant temperature, in the presence of an excess of solute (when no more solute will dissolve) the solution is said to be saturated. The solubility of a solid in a solvent is defined as the maximum number of grams of the solid that will dissolve in 1 kg (1000 g) of the solvent, in the presence of excess solid, at a given temperature.

Large quantities of water are used by industry as a solvent, and for cooling. Often very pure water is required and this may be produced by distillation, or by the removal of unwanted solutes using an ion-exchange resin.

Hardness in Water

Tap water sometimes contains magnesium or calcium salts which cause it to be described as hard water. A hard water is defined as a water that will not readily give a permanent lather with soap.

Temporary hardness is due to the presence of the hydrogen-carbonates of magnesium or calcium, and may be destroyed by heating, which causes the hydrogencarbonate to decompose.

$$Ca(HCO_3)_2(aq) \rightarrow CaCO_3(s) + H_2O(l) + CO_2(g)$$

or by adding calcium hydroxide (Clark's method)

$$Ca(OH)_2(s) + Ca(HCO_3)_2(aq) \rightarrow 2CaCO_3(s) + 2H_2O(l)$$

Permanent hardness is due to the presence of the sulphates of magnesium or calcium and cannot be destroyed by heating because these sulphates are stable to heat.

Both types of hardness are removed by passing the hard water through an ion-exchange resin, which will exchange its sodium ions for the calcium ions of the water. The solution emerging from a typical domestic water softener is thus one of sodium sulphate and/or of sodium hydrogencarbonate.

Another method of removing both types of hardness is to add sodium carbonate ($Na_2CO_3 \cdot 10H_2O$ is 'washing soda') which will precipitate calcium carbonate as a fine white powder.

$$Ca(HCO_3)_2(aq) + Na_2CO_3(aq \text{ or } s) \rightarrow CaCO_3(s)$$
$$+ 2NaHCO_3(aq)$$

$$CaSO_4(aq) + Na_2CO_3(aq \text{ or } s) \rightarrow CaCO_3(s)$$
$$+ Na_2SO_4(aq)$$

The remaining solution lathers readily with soap and the suspension of calcium carbonate is easily removed by rinsing laundry. Distillation is a third method of removing both types of hardness from water.

Industry and the Environment

The siting of industry in Britain is important, and is generally not accidental. An oil refinery and industries dependent on its products are likely to be sited on the coast, whether the oil comes from the North Sea or from abroad. Many industries are sited along the Cheshire–Lancashire border because of the availability of Cheshire salt, Lancashire coal and Derbyshire limestone. The steel industry has several major centres, (the Clyde valley, Cleveland, South Wales and the Scunthorpe–Sheffield–Corby area), mostly adjacent to ports where the ore is imported. The aluminium smelters are situated on or near the coast partly because they depend on imported ore and partly because aluminium production requires large quantities of electrical energy.

Factories have to be sited close to centres of population, or population centres have to grow near to the factories, so that a work force is readily available. Many factories need supplies of water for cleaning or for cooling purposes, and such factories need to be sited by a river if they are not in a coastal area. When goods have been manufactured, they need to be sold, and the site of the industry may also depend on the availability of markets.

We depend on industry for the creation of much of our wealth. The chemical industry can be described as $5-10-15-30$: it employs 5% of Britain's workers, it produces 10% of our industrial output, it has about 15% of our industrial plant, and it produces about 30% of our export surplus in manufactured goods. Some of the most important products of the British chemical industry are synthetic fibres, soaps and soapless detergents, rubbers, paints, plastics, pharmaceuticals, fertilizers, insecticides, metals and alloys, transistors, silicon chips, sulphuric acid, chlorine and glass.

Cyclic Processes

Nature has many *cyclic processes*. For example, the combustion of fuels gives carbon dioxide which is taken up by plants in photosynthesis, the plants may be eaten, respiration produces carbon dioxide again, and plants may yield fossil fuels such as coal and natural gas. The nitrogen cycle is another example. In this case man intervenes by supplying fertilizers to plants.

About half of the steel made in Britain each year is based on scrap iron and about half comes from iron ores processed in blast furnaces. Other metals such as copper, nickel, lead and zinc are recycled on a smaller scale. Man's efforts to recycle materials are not as successful as nature's, however, and much of our rubbish has to be disposed of by burying it on land or at sea.

Pollution

This can be defined as any unwanted substance in an objectionable proportion in a wanted place. The pollutant may not be actively poisonous, but it may give offence to one or more of our five senses (sight, smell, taste, touch or hearing). Hence noise and the release of energy can also be considered to be pollutants.

Much of the pollution of the air is as a result of energy conversion. Incomplete combustion of fuels results in carbon monoxide or smoke (finely divided carbon particles) escaping into the air we breathe. Oil and coal contain a very small proportion of sulphur which, during combustion, produces sulphur dioxide. Rain falling through the atmosphere dissolves this gas and becomes more acidic than it would have been in an atmosphere containing the normal amount of naturally occurring carbon dioxide. This extra acidity may affect our lungs; fish and plant life may suffer and our buildings may slowly disintegrate. We may enjoy travelling by car, but the petrol engine causes some oxides of nitrogen to be released into the atmosphere (again making it acidic) as well as polluting the air with lead compounds which are poisonous.

Sewage and detergents from our homes and factories often cause water to be polluted. If the farmer spreads too much fertilizer on his fields, and it rains more heavily than he anticipates, nitrates and phosphates may be washed through the soil and into our drinking water supplies. The excessive growth of plants in rivers and lakes may cause oxygen starvation which affects fish and the natural decay of materials in the water. Water may also be polluted by effluents, such as acids, alkalis, and solutions of metallic salts used in electrolysis, from factories. Strict controls are needed to ensure that the water in our taps is fit to drink, and the water used by or disposed of by industry is of known purity.

Radioactive Substances

Some materials are radioactive, i.e. the nuclei of the atoms of some of the elements in them are spontaneously unstable, and they break down, or decay, producing different elements, and causing the properties of the material to change. Along with the formation of new materials, radioactive decay may be accompanied by the production of α-particles (helium nuclei, absorbed by paper or thin aluminium foil), β-particles (electrons, stopped by glass) or γ-rays (photons, the intensity of which is only reduced by thick sheets of lead).

Nuclear reactions are independent of temperature, but often produce large quantities of heat. The rate at which radioactive decay occurs is measured in terms of its half-life, $t_{1/2}$, which is the time taken for the radioactivity to decrease to half of its initial value. For example:

$$^{234}_{92}U \rightarrow {}^{230}_{90}Th;\ t_{1/2} = 2 \times 10^5 \text{ years}$$

$$^{212}_{92}Pb \rightarrow {}^{212}_{93}Bi;\ t_{1/2} = 10.6 \text{ hours}$$

Radioactive materials are used in medicine (e.g. in the treatment of cancer), in measuring the thickness of materials, as tracers, in measuring the solubility of sparingly soluble substances such as lead(II) chloride, for investigating reaction mechanisms and for food sterilization. They are also used in power generation (about one sixth of our electricity comes from nuclear power stations), and in the production of weapons.

The disposal of radioactive materials and safety standards where they are used are matters of national and international concern. Many such materials take a very long time to decay before they become safe, and their effect on the human body can be horrific. Control is needed to ensure that neither nuclear accidents nor nuclear warfare ever occur.

Questions

1   In the Middle East drinking water is scarce and sea water is often processed for drinking. Which one of the following processes is likely to provide the *best* method of converting sea water into drinking water of acceptable purity?

A   ion exchange
B   distillation
C   filtration
D   chromatography
E   centrifugation

2 Which of the following, found as minerals, will dissolve in rain water, thus making it into a 'hard water'?

A   sodium nitrate
B   potassium chloride
C   magnesium sulphate
D   aluminium oxide
E   lead(II) carbonate

3 Which of the following pollutants in a river is *not* biodegradable and thus will not simply rot away?

A   a paper bag
B   orange peel
C   an apple core
D   a plastic box
E   a slice of bread

4 Which of the following non-metals will react with steam at a high temperature?

A   carbon
B   nitrogen
C   oxygen
D   sulphur
E   chlorine

5 Which of these substances would be regarded as a serious pollutant if much was found in domestic drinking water?

A   calcium sulphate
B   sodium nitrate
C   calcium hydrogencarbonate
D   magnesium sulphate
E   oxygen

6 Which of the following substances is regarded seriously as a pollutant in air?

A   carbon dioxide
B   water vapour
C   sulphur dioxide
D   argon
E   methane

7 The following graph shows how the solubility of calcium hydroxide changes with change in temperature.

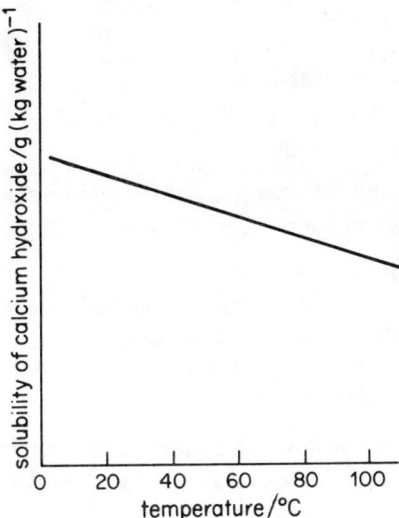

When a saturated solution of calcium hydroxide in water, in contact with excess solid, is cooled from 100°C to 20°C, which of the following will occur?

A The quantity of solid calcium hydroxide present increases.

B The quantity of solid calcium hydroxide present decreases.

C The quantity of solid calcium hydroxide present remains constant.

D Crystals of ice start to form at the top of the solution.

E The result depends on whether the calcium hydroxide is in the form of large lumps or a fine powder.

8 Which of the following fertilizers represented by chemical formulae contains the greatest proportion (by mass) of nitrogen?

A $NH_4H_2PO_4$

B NH_3

C $(NH_4)_2SO_4$

D $CO(NH_2)_2$

E $Ca(NO_3)_2$

9 In which of the following ways does the solubility of a salt in water usually vary as the temperature increases?

    A it decreases
    B it increases
    C it decreases, then increases
    D it increases, then decreases
    E it stays the same

10 Which of the following statements about air provides evidence to suggest that air is a mixture?

    A its composition is variable
    B it contains 20% oxygen and 80% nitrogen
    C dry air does not cause rusting
    D carbon dioxide is used in photosynthesis
    E it is soluble in water

11 Which of the following plastic materials, if it is burnt as a means of disposal, is the greatest pollutant of the air?

    A poly(ethene) or polythene
    B poly(propene) or polypropylene
    C poly(phenylethene) or polystrene
    D poly(chloroethene) or polyvinylchloride or pvc
    E Perspex

12 Which of the following pollutants of the air will *not* be washed away by rain water?

    A sulphur dioxide
    B nitrogen dioxide
    C hydrogen sulphide
    D hydrogen chloride
    E tetraethyllead

13 What colour change will occur when water is added to anhydrous copper(II) sulphate?

    A white to blue
    B blue to white
    C pink to blue
    D blue to pink
    E purple to colourless

14 Which of the following substances will soften drinking
water without causing a precipitate to form?

 A calcium hydroxide
 B sodium carbonate
 C cation exchange resin
 D anion exchange resin
 E a detergent

15 9 g of sodium chloride when dissolved in water gives 34 g
of a saturated solution at 20°C. The solubility of sodium
chloride (calculated in grams per 1000 g of solvent) at this
temperature is

 A 300
 B 330
 C 360
 D 390
 E 420

Select the appropriate response from the following list of
chemicals for *questions 16–20*.

 A carbon monoxide
 B nitrogen monoxide
 C sulphur dioxide
 D tetraethyllead
 E methane

Which of these responses best describes the following ways in
which pollutants may be formed

16 a colourless gas, with a pungent smell, which is released
together with carbon dioxide when coal burns?

17 a colourless gas which turns brown in air and is formed on
'hot spots' in a car engine?

18 a gas released when vegetation rots?

19 a substance which is put into petrol to improve its octane
rating?

20 a gas which is released when natural gas burns in a water
heater which is not adequately ventilated?

Select the appropriate response from the following list of metals for *questions 21—25*.

A copper
B magnesium
C sodium
D zinc
E iron

Which of these responses best describes a metal which

21 burns in air, giving out an orange light?

22 is a silver-coloured solid that becomes a white powder when left out in the air. This white powder when treated with hydrochloric acid gives a colourless gas which is not flammable?

23 reacts reversibly with steam according to the general equation

metal + steam $\rightleftharpoons$ metal oxide + hydrogen?

24 on heating in air gives a compound that will dissolve both in hot concentrated sodium hydroxide solution and in concentrated hydrochloric acid?

25 burns in air producing solid residue which yields oxygen when treated with water?

10 Metals

Metals are electropositive elements that tend to form
compounds by the loss of electrons, producing positive ions. At
room temperature, all metals (except mercury, a liquid) are
solids which tend to have shiny surfaces, and conduct
electricity. Metals are often malleable (they can be beaten or
rolled into sheets) and ductile (they can be made into wires
which are strong, i.e. they have a high tensile strength).

The Activity Series

The most reactive metals are found on the left side of the
Periodic Table. The activity, or reactivity series is a list of
metals in order of decreasing reactivity towards oxygen (as air),
water or steam, and dilute hydrochloric acid. The series also
indicates which metals will displace others from solutions of the
latter's salts, and which metal oxides will be reduced by
hydrogen or carbon.

The activity may be measured in terms of voltages, and the
series is then called the electrochemical series. The order of
elements is as follows:

Potassium⎫	
Calcium ⎬	Group I and II metals
Sodium ⎪	
Magnesium⎭	
Aluminium	Group III
CARBON → Zinc⎫	d-block metals
Iron⎭	
Lead	Group IV
→ Hydrogen	The standard element
Copper⎫	more d-block elements
Silver⎭	

The oxides of copper and silver (below hydrogen in the series) will be reduced to the metal by hydrogen. For example,

$$CuO + H_2 \rightarrow Cu + H_2O$$

Carbon is a more vigorous reducing agent than hydrogen and will reduce the oxides of several metals above hydrogen in the series. Copper is below zinc in the series and will not displace zinc from a solution containing zinc ions. However, the reverse process will occur, i.e. zinc will displace copper from a solution containing copper ions.

$$Cu^{2+}(aq) + Zn(s) \rightarrow Zn^{2+}(aq) + Cu(s)$$

Coloured Metal Ions

In the above reaction, a solution containing $Cu^{2+}(aq)$ ions is blue, while that containing $Zn^{2+}(aq)$ is colourless. Many transition metals have ions that are coloured in aqueous solution. Some of the common ions with their colours in aqueous solutions are listed in the following table.

Metal	Formula of ion	Colour
chromium	$Cr^{3+}(aq)$	blue-green
manganese	$Mn^{2+}(aq)$	very pale pink
iron	$Fe^{2+}(aq)$	pale green
	$Fe^{3+}(aq)$	yellow or brown
copper	$Cu^{2+}(aq)$	blue

In aqueous solution, hydrogen, ammonium, sodium, potassium, magnesium, calcium, barium, aluminium, zinc, lead(II) and silver ions are colourless.

The Flame Test

One of the ways by which some metal ions can be identified is by the colouration produced when a compound containing the ion is put in a flame. Common flame colourations are shown in the following table.

Metal ion	Flame colouration
Li^+	bright red
Ca^{2+}	orange-red (dark red)
Na^+	orange-yellow (bright)
Cu^{2+}	green and blue
Ba^{2+}	light green
K^+	lilac

The Metal Hydroxides

Group I hydroxides are soluble in water, giving alkalis. Group II hydroxides increase in solubility with increase in atomic number of the metal.

The hydroxides of metals such as zinc and aluminium are amphoteric. When solutions containing many hydroxide ions are added to aqueous solutions containing these metal ions, the insoluble hydroxide is first precipitated and, in the presence of an excess of hydroxide ions, the precipitate dissolves (as a complex anion). For example,

$$Al^{3+}(aq) + 3OH^-(aq) \rightarrow Al(OH)_3(s)$$

$$Al(OH)_3(s) + 3OH^-(aq) \rightarrow Al(OH)_6^{3-}(aq)$$

These precipitated hydroxides are soluble *also* in acids. For example,

$$Al(OH)_3(s) + 3H^+(aq) \rightarrow Al^{3+}(aq) + 3H_2O(l)$$

Transition metal ions produce many coloured insoluble hydroxides, and this may assist in the identification of these metals. When aqueous ammonia is used as the source of hydroxide ions, the precipitate often dissolves due to the formation of complex cations. For example,

$$Cu^{2+}(aq) \quad + 2OH^-(aq) \rightarrow Cu(OH)_2(s)$$
$$Cu(OH)_2(s) \quad + 4NH_3(aq) \rightarrow Cu(NH_3)_4^{2+}(aq)$$
$$+ 2OH^-(aq)$$

In this example a deep blue solution results due to the formation of the complex tetraamminecopper(II) ion, $Cu(NH_3)_4^{2+}(aq)$.

The hydroxides of the more reactive metals are unaffected by heat, but those of the less reactive metals, e.g. copper hydroxide, are converted into the oxide by heating.

$$Cu(OH)_2(s) \rightarrow CuO(s) + H_2O(l)$$

The result of adding aqueous solutions of sodium hydroxide and ammonia to solutions containing various common metal ions is summarized in the following table:

Solution of salt containing ions of	With a little sodium hydroxide solution	With an excess of sodium hydroxide solution	With a little aqueous ammonia	With an excess of aqueous ammonia
sodium	—	—	—	—
potassium	—	—	—	—
ammonium	on warming gives ammonia	on warming gives ammonia	—	—
magnesium	white precipitate	no change	white precipitate	no change
calcium	white precipitate	no change	—	—
aluminium	white precipitate	colourless solution	white precipitate	no change
lead(II)	white precipitate	colourless solution	white precipitate	no change
iron(II)	'green' precipitate	no change	'green' precipitate	no change
iron(III)	red-brown precipitate	no change	red-brown precipitate	no change
copper(II)	pale blue precipitate	no change	pale blue precipitate	deep blue solution
zinc	white precipitate	colourless solution	white precipitate	colourless solution

The Metal Carbonates

Group I carbonates are soluble in water, and are alkaline because of hydrolysis.

Group II carbonates are insoluble in water but dissolve in

dilute solutions of carbonic acid, producing the metal hydrogencarbonate. When carbon dioxide is passed into lime water (calcium hydroxide solution) it turns chalky (calcium carbonate is precipitated) and then clears (soluble calcium hydrogencarbonate is formed).

$$Ca(OH)_2(aq) + CO_2(aq) \rightarrow CaCO_3(s) + H_2O(l)$$
$$CaCO_3(s) + CO_2(aq) + H_2O(l) \rightarrow Ca(HCO_3)_2(aq)$$

d-block metal carbonates are insoluble in water, and are often coloured. Zinc is a d-block element but not a transition element: its carbonate is white but insoluble in water.

The carbonates of Group I metals are unaffected by heat, but other carbonates decompose on heating to produce the oxide. For example,

$$CaCO_3(s) \rightarrow CaO(s) + CO_2(g)$$

The Extraction of Metals

Iron is produced industrially in a blast furnace. By sintering, the ore is converted to iron(II) diiron(III) oxide, Fe_3O_4, and then it is mixed with carbon (coke) and limestone. The carbon burns in a blast of hot air forming first carbon dioxide and then carbon monoxide.

$$C + O_2 \rightarrow CO_2$$
$$CO_2 + C \rightarrow 2CO$$

Then the oxide is reduced by carbon monoxide (and by carbon).

$$Fe_3O_4 + 4CO \rightleftharpoons 3Fe + 4CO_2$$

The limestone decomposes and then combines with earthy impurities.

$$CaCO_3 \rightarrow CaO + CO_2$$
$$CaO + SiO_2 \rightarrow CaSiO_3$$

The main products of the process are molten slag ($CaSiO_3$) and molten iron which form two layers at the base of the furnace. The gases emerging from the top of the furnace contain enough surplus carbon monoxide to enable them to be burnt to heat the ingoing air. The iron produced in a blast furnace contains several impurities, mainly carbon which makes it too brittle for many purposes. Steel is mainly iron and it contains less than 1.5 % of carbon. To convert iron into steel, the molten iron is put in a basic oxygen converter and a jet of oxygen directed at its surface. The oxidation of the impurities, including the carbon, is so exothermic that it keeps the whole mixture molten. Alloying elements, e.g. manganese, vanadium and tungsten, may then be added.

Aluminium is extracted from the ore bauxite, $Al_2O_3 \cdot 2H_2O$, which is crushed and dissolved in a hot concentrated solution of sodium hydroxide under pressure (Bayer process). Cooling and seeding of the resulting solution causes the formation of aluminium hydroxide which is heated to give pure aluminium oxide.

$$2Al(OH)_3(s) \rightarrow Al_2O_3(s) + 3H_2O(g)$$

The purified oxide is dissolved in molten cryolite (Na_3AlF_6) which is electrolysed between graphite electrodes. Oxygen is liberated at the anode which burns away to carbon monoxide and carbon dioxide. Aluminium is liberated at the cathode and is siphoned out every few hours (Hall–Héroult cell).

Sodium is also manufactured by electrolysis. The electrolysis takes place in the Downs' Cell, in which the electrolyte is a molten mixture of sodium chloride and calcium chloride at 600°C (calcium chloride reduces the melting point of the sodium chloride). Sodium is produced at the steel cathode, and chlorine at the carbon (graphite) anode.

Alloys

A homogeneous mixture of two or more metals is called an alloy. Brass, for example, is a mixture containing 60 % copper and 40 % zinc, and 'H30' is a light-weight high-strength alloy containing 97 % aluminium, and about 1 % each of magnesium, silicon and manganese. Different solders (jointing alloys) contain different proportions of tin and lead, and are useful because of their low melting points, e.g. a solder of 70 % tin and 30 % lead melts over the range 183–195°C.

Alloys containing mercury are called amalgams. For example, sodium dissolves in mercury giving a mixture called

sodium amalgam (as at the cathode of a Castner–Kellner–
Solvay cell, see pages 35 and 104).

One of the most important alloys is steel which is iron
containing a controlled, low proportion of carbon. The quality
of a steel depends on the carbon content. Mild steels (up to
0.25 % C) are soft: they are used for wires, rivets, sheets, and
for general engineering purposes. Medium-carbon steels (0.25 –
0.45 % C) are used in the manufacture of springs, and high-
carbon steels (0.45 – 1.5 % C) are hard, being used for hammers
and chisels. Stainless steel contains 74 % iron, 18 % chromium
and 8 % nickel.

Questions

1 Which of the following ions (in a compound) gives a
  dark red colour in a flame test?

  A calcium
  B barium
  C potassium
  D lithium
  E copper

2 When iron is produced in a blast furnace, which of the
  following reactions, represented by chemical equations,
  does *not* occur?

  A C $+O_2$ $\rightarrow CO_2$
  B CO_2 $+C$ $\rightarrow 2CO$
  C $4CO$ $+Fe_3O_4$ $\rightarrow 3Fe + 4CO_2$
  D $2CO$ $+O_2$ $\rightarrow 2CO_2$
  E $CaCO_3$ $+SiO_2$ $\rightarrow CaSiO_3 + CO_2$

3 Which of the following describes accurately one of the
  steps in the extraction of aluminium from impure
  aluminium oxide (bauxite)?

  A the bauxite is dissolved in cryolite
  B the temperature is about 1000 °C
  C the anode is made of carbon (graphite) and the
     cathode of iron
  D the cathode burns away
  E aluminium is released at the anode

4   Which of the following substances would be changed
    after heating and then cooling in air?

    A   lead(II) nitrate
    B   sodium chloride
    C   copper(II) oxide
    D   calcium chloride
    E   zinc oxide

5   Which of the following nitrates will yield the metal if it is
    heated?

    A   sodium nitrate
    B   silver nitrate
    C   lead(II) nitrate
    D   copper(II) nitrate
    E   calcium nitrate

6   Which of the following alloys contains the *highest*
    proportion of carbon?

    A   mild steel
    B   brass
    C   solder
    D   duralumin
    E   nichrome

7   Which of the following metal chlorides is the *least* soluble
    in water?

    A   sodium chloride
    B   barium chloride
    C   iron(III) chloride
    D   silver chloride
    E   copper(II) chloride

8   Which of the following substances will *not* yield
    copper(II) sulphate when it is added to dilute sulphuric
    acid?

    A   copper
    B   copper(II) oxide
    C   copper(II) hydroxide
    D   copper(II) carbonate
    E   tetraamminecopper(II) hydroxide

9 Which of the following compounds is *not* amphoteric?

   A   aluminium oxide
   B   zinc oxide
   C   lead(II) oxide
   D   copper(II) oxide
   E   zinc hydroxide

10 Which of the following metals will *not* displace copper when added to an aqueous solution of copper(II) sulphate?

   A   zinc
   B   iron
   C   magnesium
   D   silver
   E   aluminium

11 Which of the following elements does *not* react according to its position in the activity/electrochemical series because it gains an oxide film on exposure to air?

   A   sodium
   B   aluminium
   C   iron
   D   lead
   E   copper

12 Which of the following metal carbonates is the *most* stable to heat?

   A   calcium carbonate
   B   sodium carbonate
   C   magnesium carbonate
   D   zinc carbonate
   E   copper(II) carbonate

13 When iron is in contact with certain metals it becomes resistant to corrosion. Which of the following metals will protect iron in this way?

   A   silver
   B   tin
   C   magnesium
   D   chromium
   E   nickel

14 Which of the following metal sulphates is the *least* soluble in water?

    A   aluminium sulphate
    B   barium sulphate
    C   copper(II) sulphate
    D   magnesium sulphate
    E   sodium sulphate

15 Which of the following metal oxides is the *least* stable to heat?

    A   iron(III) oxide
    B   calcium oxide
    C   zinc oxide
    D   lead(IV) oxide
    E   sodium oxide

Select the appropriate response from the following descriptions of precipitates for *questions 16–20.*

    A   a red-brown precipitate, insoluble in excess aqueous ammonia
    B   a white precipitate, soluble in excess aqueous ammonia producing a colourless solution
    C   a white precipitate, insoluble in excess aqueous ammonia
    D   a pale blue precipitate, soluble in excess aqueous ammonia to give a deep blue solution
    E   a white (often 'dirty green') precipitate, soluble in excess aqueous ammonia

Which of these responses *best* describes the result that will be observed when aqueous ammonia is added slowly, until it is present in excess, to aqueous solutions containing the following ions?

16 iron(II)

17 copper(II)

18 aluminium

19 zinc

20 iron(III)

Select the appropriate response from the following descriptions
of precipitates for *questions 21—25*.

A   a white precipitate, insoluble in excess aqueous
      sodium hydroxide solution

B   a white precipitate, soluble in excess aqueous sodium
      hydroxide solution giving a colourless solution

C   a red-brown precipitate, insoluble in excess aqueous
      sodium hydroxide solution

D   a blue precipitate, insoluble in excess aqueous sodium
      hydroxide solution

E   no precipitate is observed

Which of these responses *best* describes what will be observed
when aqueous sodium hydroxide solution is added slowly,
until it is present in excess, to aqueous solutions containing the
following metal ions?

21   potassium

22   magnesium

23   copper(II)

24   iron(III)

25   zinc

11 Non-metals

Non-metals are electronegative elements which tend to gain electrons in compound formation forming ionic compounds with metals and covalent compounds with one another. They are found towards the right-hand side of the Periodic Table.

The Preparation of Common Gases

Hydrogen is prepared by the action of dilute hydrochloric acid (or sulphuric acid) on zinc. A few drops of copper(II) sulphate solution speed up the reaction and the hydrogen, which is less dense than air, may be collected over water. (Collection of hydrogen by upward delivery is possible but there is no way of telling when a vessel is full.)

$$Zn(s) + 2HCl(aq) \rightarrow ZnCl_2(aq) + H_2(g)$$

Hydrogen may also be prepared by the electrolysis of dilute sulphuric acid (see page 35), and by the reaction between water and very reactive metals (see page 76).

Carbon monoxide may be prepared by passing carbon dioxide over hot carbon. Surplus carbon dioxide is absorbed in concentrated sodium hydroxide solution and the carbon monoxide collected over water. Carbon monoxide cannot be collected by displacement of air: it has about the same density.

$$CO_2(g) + C(s) \rightarrow 2CO(g)$$
$$NaOH(aq) + CO_2(g) \rightarrow NaHCO_3(aq)$$

Carbon dioxide is prepared by the action of dilute hydrochloric acid on marble chips (calcium carbonate).

$$CaCO_3(s) + 2HCl(aq) \rightarrow CaCl_2(aq) + H_2O(l) + CO_2(g)$$

The gas is denser than air and may be collected by downward delivery or over water, in which it is only moderately soluble.

Nitrogen may be prepared by heating a mixture of the concentrated solutions of ammonium chloride and sodium nitrite. In ionic terms, the reaction is

$$NH_4^+(aq) + NO_2^-(aq) \rightarrow 2H_2O(l) + N_2(g)$$

Nitrogen may also be obtained from the air by removing the other gases (see page 75). The nitrogen obtained in this way is contaminated with the noble gases. Nitrogen is usually collected over water; it cannot be collected by displacement of air.

Ammonia gas is obtained by heating a mixture of solid ammonium chloride and solid calcium hydroxide.

$$2NH_4Cl(s) + Ca(OH)_2(s) \rightarrow CaCl_2(s) + 2H_2O(l) + 2NH_3(g)$$

Traces of water are removed by drying with calcium oxide, and, because ammonia is less dense than air, it may be collected by upward delivery. If a solution is required the inverted funnel technique must be used.

Alternative reagents are any other ammonium salt (e.g. the sulphate), and sodium hydroxide (this alkali is usually used in solution). Ammonia is the only common alkaline gas.

Oxygen may be prepared from moderately concentrated hydrogen peroxide solution by adding manganese(IV) oxide as a catalyst.

$$2H_2O_2(aq) \rightarrow 2H_2O(l) + O_2(g)$$

Alternatively it may be prepared by heating potassium chlorate(V) with manganese(IV) oxide as a catalyst.

$$2KClO_3(s) \rightarrow 2KCl(s) + O_2(g)$$

The oxygen may be collected over water; it cannot be collected by displacement of air.

Hydrogen sulphide is obtained when moderately concentrated hydrochloric acid reacts with iron(II) sulphide.

$$FeS(s) + 2HCl(aq) \rightarrow FeCl_2(aq) + H_2S(g)$$

The gas may be collected over water, in which it is only moderately soluble.

Sulphur dioxide is prepared by the action of hot concentrated sulphuric acid on copper turnings.

$$Cu(s) + 2H_2SO_4(aq) \rightarrow CuSO_4(aq) + 2H_2O(l) + SO_2(g)$$

Alternatively, solid sodium sulphite may be warmed with dilute sulphuric acid.

$$Na_2SO_3(s) + H_2SO_4(aq) \rightarrow Na_2SO_4(aq) + H_2O(l) + SO_2(g)$$

The gas may be collected by downward delivery.

Chlorine may be obtained by the action of concentrated hydrochloric acid on manganese(IV) oxide (with heating), or potassium manganate(VII) (in the cold).

$$MnO_2(s) + 4HCl(aq) \rightarrow MnCl_2(aq) + 2H_2O(l) + Cl_2(g)$$

$$2KMnO_4(s) + 16HCl(aq) \rightarrow 2KCl(aq) + 2MnCl_2(aq)$$
$$+ 8H_2O(l) + 5Cl_2(g)$$

The gas is usually passed through water to remove traces of hydrogen chloride, then through concentrated calcium chloride solution (acting as a drying agent). Chlorine may be collected by downward delivery because it is denser than air or, if it is not required dry, over water (the addition of common salt lowers its solubility).

Hydrogen chloride is prepared by adding concentrated sulphuric acid to solid sodium chloride.

$$NaCl(s) + H_2SO_4(l) \rightarrow NaHSO_4(s) + HCl(g)$$

It is usually collected by downward delivery. If a solution is required the inverted funnel technique must be used.

Testing for Gases

Some of the tests used to identify common gases are shown in the following table.

Gas	Test	Acid/Alkali
hydrogen	burns with an explosive pop forms moisture	neutral
carbon monoxide	burns quietly and *then* turns calcium hydroxide solution chalky	neutral
carbon dioxide	turns calcium hydroxide solution (lime water) chalky	weakly acidic
nitrogen	does not burn nor support combustion of a splint; does not affect calcium hydroxide solution	neutral

Gas	Test	Acid/ Alkali
ammonia	(a) produces a blue-white smoke with hydrogen chloride (b) turns damp red litmus paper to blue (c) characteristic smell	alkaline
nitrogen dioxide	brown fumes (not to be confused with bromine); characteristic smell	acidic
oxygen	relights a glowing splint	neutral
steam (water)	(a) turns white anhydrous copper(II) sulphate to blue (b) turns blue anhydrous cobalt(II) chloride to pink (c) condenses at $100\,^{\circ}$C (purity test)	neutral
hydrogen sulphide	turns colourless lead(II) nitrate solution to a silver-black solid; characteristic smell (bad eggs)	weakly acidic
sulphur dioxide	turns orange potassium dichromate solution to blue-green; characteristic smell	acidic
chlorine	pale yellow-green gas, turns moist blue litmus paper to red then bleaches it; characteristic smell	acidic
hydrogen chloride	produces a blue-white smoke with ammonia gas; characteristic smell	acidic
bromine	red-brown fumes, turns damp blue litmus paper to red then slowly bleaches it; characteristic smell	acidic
iodine	purple vapour (sublimation)	neutral

Testing for Anions

Some simple tests used in analysis to indicate the presence of some common acid radicals are shown in the following table:

Anion	Formula	Test
carbonate	CO_3^{2-}	dilute hydrochloric acid produces carbon dioxide (test with calcium hydroxide solution)
nitrate	NO_3^-	(a) warming with aqueous sodium hydroxide and Devarda's alloy produces ammonia (smell, etc) (b) to a cold solution add dilute sulphuric acid, iron(II) sulphate solution and then concentrated sulphuric acid: a brown ring is produced
sulphide	S^{2-}	dilute hydrochloric acid produces hydrogen sulphide (smell and test with lead(II) nitrate solution)
sulphite	SO_3^{2-}	dilute hydrochloric acid produces sulphur dioxide (smell and test with potassium dichromate solution)
sulphate	SO_4^{2-}	dilute hydrochloric acid and aqueous barium chloride solution gives white precipitate of barium sulphate
chloride	Cl^-	(a) silver nitrate solution, in presence of dilute nitric acid, gives white precipitate of silver chloride (soluble in aqueous ammonia) (b) concentrated sulphuric acid on warming gives hydrogen chloride (test with ammonia)

Anion	Formula	Test
bromide	Br^-	(a) silver nitrate solution, in presence of dilute nitric acid gives pale yellow precipitate of silver bromide (b) concentrated sulphuric acid on warming gives a mixture of hydrogen bromide and bromine (red-brown gas, characteristic smell)
iodide	I^-	(a) silver nitrate solution, in presence of dilute nitric acid, gives yellow precipitate of silver iodide (b) concentrated sulphuric acid on warming gives a mixture of hydrogen iodide and iodine (purple vapour, characteristic smell)

Some Important Industrial Preparations

Sulphur is extracted using the Frasch process. Superheated water (above 100°C but still a liquid) melts the sulphur, and hot, compressed air forces it to the earth's surface in the form of a foam, from which the sulphur solidifies.

Ammonia is produced by reacting hydrogen with nitrogen in the presence of an iron catalyst at 400−500 °C and at 20−35 MPa.

$$N_2(g) + 3H_2(g) \rightleftharpoons 2NH_3(g); \qquad \Delta H = -92 \, kJ/mol$$

The hydrogen for this process is obtained by the steam reforming of naphtha, and the nitrogen is obtained from the air (in secondary reformers). *Nitric acid* is produced industrially from ammonia in the Ostwald process. Ammonia is oxidized by air in the presence of a platinum catalyst.

$$4NH_3(g) + 5O_2(g) \rightarrow 4NO(g) + 6H_2O(l)$$

The nitrogen monoxide combines with excess oxygen to produce nitrogen dioxide.

$$2NO(g) + O_2(g) \rightarrow 2NO_2(g)$$

Then the nitrogen dioxide is dissolved in water in the presence of more oxygen.

$$4NO_2(g) + 2H_2O(l) + O_2(g) \rightarrow 4HNO_3(aq)$$

Sulphuric acid is obtained by the Contact process. Sulphur is burnt to give sulphur dioxide and then passed, with more air, over vanadium(V) oxide (the catalyst) at 450°C.

$$S(s) + O_2(g) \rightarrow SO_2(g)$$

$$2SO_2(g) + O_2(g) \rightarrow 2SO_3(g); \quad \Delta H - 188 \text{ kJ/mol}$$

The sulphur trioxide produced is dissolved in some concentrated sulphuric acid which is then poured into water to produce a greater quantity of concentrated sulphuric acid.

$$SO_3(g) + H_2O(l) \rightarrow H_2SO_4(l)$$

Chlorine and sodium hydroxide solution (with some hydrogen) are manufactured by electrolysis. In the Castner–Kellner–Solvay process or mercury cathode brine cell and soda cell process, concentrated sodium chloride solution is electrolysed between a graphite anode and a flowing mercury cathode. Chlorine is released at the anode and sodium amalgam forms at the cathode.

$$2Cl^-(aq) \rightarrow Cl_2(g) + 2e^-$$

$$Na^+(aq) + e^- \rightarrow Na(\text{in Hg})$$

The sodium amalgam runs into a second trough (or a tower) where it reacts with water in the presence of graphite grids.

$$2Na(\text{in Hg}) + 2H_2O(l) \rightarrow 2NaOH(aq) + H_2(g)$$

The mercury returns to the electrolytic cell.

The alternative process uses a diaphragm cell. Again chlorine is produced at a graphite anode. However, only some of the sodium chloride solution is converted into sodium hydroxide solution after flowing through the diaphragm to the steel cathode. The mixture produced at the cathode (where hydrogen is also liberated) is warmed and sodium chloride crystallizes out, leaving concentrated sodium hydroxide solution.

Questions

1 Which of the following gases turns litmus or a universal indicator to red, and then bleaches it?

A   chlorine
B   water vapour or steam
C   ammonia
D   hydrogen chloride
E   sulphur dioxide

2 Which of the following gases would give a silver-black precipitate with a solution of lead(II) ions?

A   hydrogen
B   hydrogen sulphide
C   hydrogen chloride
D   ammonia
E   oxygen

3 Dilute nitric acid, followed by some silver nitrate solution, is added to a solution containing a sodium salt. If a white precipitate is produced it indicates that the sodium salt present is the

A   chloride.
B   bromide.
C   iodide.
D   carbonate.
E   sulphate.

4 The colour of the vapour produced when a bromide is heated with manganese(IV) oxide and concentrated sulphuric acid is

A   yellow-green.
B   red-brown.
C   violet-black.
D   blue-black.
E   blue-green.

5 When elements in Group VI of the Periodic Table
   combine to produce electrovalent compounds, they form
   ions with the following charge

   A   2+
   B   2−
   C   4+
   D   6+
   E   6−

6 The colour of iodine vapour is

   A   red.
   B   yellow.
   C   green.
   D   brown.
   E   purple.

7 Which of the following gases may *not* be collected over
   water?

   A   hydrogen sulphide
   B   hydrogen chloride
   C   chlorine
   D   carbon dioxide
   E   carbon monoxide

8 Which of the following chemicals will *not* give oxygen on
   heating?

   A   hydrogen peroxide
   B   potassium chlorate(V)
   C   sodium nitrate
   D   calcium carbonate
   E   potassium manganate(VII)

9 Which of the following, when burning, reacts with the
   nitrogen in the air?
   A   a splint
   B   a candle
   C   methane
   D   magnesium
   E   phosphorus

10 The systematic name for sodium hypochlorite, NaOCl, is

    A   sodium chlorate(I).
    B   sodium chlorate(III).
    C   sodium chlorate(V).
    D   sodium chlorate(VII).
    E   sodium hydrogenchlorate.

11 Which bad-smelling gas escapes from rotten eggs?

    A   chlorine
    B   hydrogen chloride
    C   hydrogen sulphide
    D   sulphur dioxide
    E   nitrogen dioxide

12 Which of the following reactions does *not* produce hydrogen?

    A   copper plus water
    B   iron plus dilute hydrochloric acid
    C   zinc plus aqueous sodium hydroxide
    D   magnesium plus steam
    E   water plus sodium hydride

13 Which of the following calcium salts would produce a brown gas on *gentle* heating?

    A   calcium bromide
    B   calcium nitrate
    C   calcium carbonate
    D   calcium chloride
    E   calcium sulphate

14 When sulphur dioxide reacts with an acidified solution of potassium dichromate the colour change is from

    A   purple to colourless.
    B   orange to green.
    C   green to orange.
    D   blue to pink.
    E   white to blue.

15 The atomicity of ammonia gas is

    A   1
    B   2
    C   3
    D   4
    E   5

Select the appropriate response from the following list of tests for common gases for *questions 16–20*.

    A   a neutral gas which only after combustion turns calcium hydroxide solution cloudy
    B   a neutral gas which has no smell and relights a strongly glowing splint
    C   a strong-smelling gas that is alkaline to litmus
    D   a strong-smelling yellow-green gas that bleaches damp litmus
    E   a strong-smelling gas that is acidic to damp litmus and turns acidified potassium manganate(VII) from purple to colourless

Which of these responses *best* describes the test for

16 oxygen?

17 sulphur dioxide?

18 carbon monoxide?

19 ammonia?

20 chlorine?

Select the appropriate response from the following list of common reagents used in tests for ions for *questions 21–25*.

    A   dilute hydrochloric acid, followed by calcium hydroxide solution in a separate vessel
    B   barium chloride solution, followed by dilute hydrochloric acid
    C   silver nitrate solution, followed by dilute nitric acid
    D   Devarda's alloy, followed by aqueous sodium hydroxide
    E   aqueous ammonia, until present in excess

Which of these responses would be *best* for testing for a

21 carbonate?

22 nitrate?

23 sulphate?

24 chloride?

25 bromide?

12 Organic Chemistry

Organic chemistry is the study of the compounds of carbon, excluding the oxides and their simple derivatives. Carbon forms millions of different compounds because carbon atoms can form bonds with other carbon atoms, producing straight chains, branched chains or rings. In addition to carbon, organic compounds may contain hydrogen, nitrogen or oxygen and occasionally phosphorus, sulphur, chlorine or other elements.

Petroleum

Petroleum (crude oil) is a dark viscous liquid which is formed underground in many parts of the world. It is a useless mixture of many useful substances. When crude oil is heated and fractionally distilled it can be separated out into dissolved gases (for fuels), gasoline (for petrol), kerosene (for paraffin), light fuel oil (for diesel oil), light lubricating oil and bitumen. All of these fractions have different boiling points, though they are still mixtures of substances requiring further processing before they can be used.

Fractional distillation of crude oil does not yield products in the proportions that the market requires, and the second stage in processing it is called catalytic cracking. Large molecules are split into small molecules at a high temperature (500 °C) using a catalyst such as aluminium oxide. Large quantities of ethene are produced in this process. Further processing stages include reforming (altering the structure of molecules) and polymerizing (making small molecules into big molecules).

Alkanes

Carbon is in Group IV of the Periodic Table. It thus has a valency of four, and is covalently bonded in most organic compounds. Carbon and hydrogen form many series of compounds called hydrocarbons. Members of the simplest of these series which contain only single bonds, are called alkanes (paraffins). The alkanes are an example of a homologous series, i.e. they are made in a similar way, their physical properties slowly alter as their molecular size increases (e.g., light molecules may be gases, heavier ones liquids, and the heaviest members of the series are likely to be solids), and their chemical properties are very similar. All alkanes have the same general formula, C_nH_{2n+2}, where n is the number of carbon atoms per molecule.

The first member of the alkane series is methane, CH_4 (natural gas). Its structure can be shown in two dimensions as

$$\begin{bmatrix} & H & \\ & | & \\ H-& C &-H \\ & | & \\ & H & \end{bmatrix}$$

In reality, the molecule is three-dimensional, and there is an angle of 109° between the bonds. A better representation of this molecule is thus

$$\begin{bmatrix} & H & \\ & | & \\ & C & \\ H \diagup & | & \diagdown H \\ & H & \end{bmatrix}$$

Three-dimensional diagrams should not be attempted unless they are vital.

The next member of the alkane series is called ethane, C_2H_6, and the third is propane, C_3H_8. Both of these molecules can have only one type of structure. However, the fourth member of the series, butane, C_4H_{10} can be represented by two distinct structural formulae, and these different forms of butane are called isomers

(normal) butane　　　2-methylpropane (isobutane)
b.p. −0.5 °C　　　b.p. −12 °C

Isomers differ in their physical properties and may also differ in their chemical properties, particularly when isomers belong to different homologous series.

Alkanes, because they contain only single bonds, are examples of saturated compounds. They often react by substitution, i.e., one or more hydrogen atoms are replaced by one or more atoms of another element (or by a radical). The lower members of the alkane series are used as fuels, because they burn liberating much heat: for example,

$$C_3H_8(g) + 5O_2(g) \rightarrow 3CO_2(g) + 4H_2O(l);$$
$$\Delta H = -2220\,kJ/mol$$

Alkenes

Another series of hydrocarbons that is important is the alkenes (olefines). Each member of this homologous series has two hydrogen atoms per molecule less than the corresponding alkane, and the general formula for alkenes is C_nH_{2n}

The lowest member of this series is ethene, C_2H_4, and in this compound the carbon atoms are linked by a double bond, i.e., four electrons are shared between the two carbon atoms. This double bond is easily broken, so alkenes are more reactive than alkanes. They react by addition to produce compounds containing single bonds, and they are said to be unsaturated. Unsaturated compounds can be identified by the following tests:

1. bromine water (red-brown) is rapidly decolourized
2. potassium manganate(VII) solution (purple) mixed with a little sodium carbonate solution is rapidly decolourized (a brown precipitate of hydrated manganese(IV) oxide is also produced).

An alkene burns readily, but the flame is more luminous and smoky than that of the corresponding alkane. Alkenes also react with hydrogen in an addition reaction producing an alkane (180 °C, nickel catalyst). This reaction (hydrogenation) is important in converting oils into fats (for food), though some people prefer their margarine to be high in polyunsaturates.

At high temperatures and pressures ethene molecules will join end to end forming poly(ethene). This substance is a polymer better known as polythene, and the process is called addition polymerization. Ethene will react in this way at room temperature and pressure (or just above these conditions) in the presence of a complex catalyst, and the product is high-density poly(ethene) which does not soften below 100 °C, so it can be sterilized. Another common polymer is polyvinyl chloride, pvc, which is made when chloroethene (vinyl chloride, C_2H_3Cl) is polymerized. Polymers of this type are all plastics, i.e. they soften on heating, can be shaped, and then on cooling they harden.

Alcohols

If a hydrogen atom in each of the alkanes is replaced by an −OH group, the homologous series of alcohols is produced, with the general formula $C_nH_{2n+1}OH$. The −OH group (or radical) is called the alcohol functional group because it often determines the way in which the molecule will react.

Methanol, CH_3OH is the first member of the series, but the most important member is the second, ethanol, C_2H_5OH. This substance is sometimes just called 'alcohol', and its production by fermentation from starches and sugars is discussed on page 68. If ethanol is required as a solvent it will have to be distilled from an excess of water. This distillation yields 'rectified spirits' which contain 96 % ethanol and 4 % water, and the last traces of water may, for example, be removed by reaction with calcium. The main way of producing ethanol for industrial purposes is by the catalytic hydration of ethene (300 °C, at 6.7 MPa, and a catalyst of phosphoric acid).

Ethanol burns in air and is sometimes used as a fuel (see page 63). Metals, such as sodium, will displace the hydrogen from the −OH radical. The oxidation of ethanol to yield other organic compounds proceeds in two stages, producing first ethanal, CH_3CHO, which has an apple-like smell, and then ethanoic acid, CH_3COOH (acetic acid or vinegar). These reactions are reversible thus:

$$C_2H_5OH \underset{\text{reduction}}{\overset{\text{oxidation}}{\rightleftharpoons}} CH_3CHO \underset{\text{reduction}}{\overset{\text{oxidation}}{\rightleftharpoons}} CH_3COOH$$

ethanol   ethanal   ethanoic acid

The oxidation can be done by using potassium dichromate and dilute sulphuric acid, or by atmospheric oxygen (wine goes sour if exposed to the air for too long).

Organic Acids

Ethanoic acid is the second member of the homologous series of carboxylic acids, which have the functional group $-COOH$, and the general formula $C_nH_{2n+1}COOH$. This functional group can be drawn as $-C\underset{O-H}{\overset{O}{\diagup}}$ to emphasize the shape and bonding. In industry ethanoic acid is made by the catalytic oxidation of butane.

Organic acids and alcohols react together to produce esters which are often used as flavours and scents. This process is called esterification and is catalysed by dilute mineral acids. The reverse of this process is hydrolysis e.g.,

$$C_2H_5OH + CH_3COOH \underset{\text{hydrolysis}}{\overset{\text{esterification}}{\rightleftharpoons}} CH_3COOC_2H_5 + H_2O$$

ethanol   ethanoic acid   ethyl ethanoate

Soaps are made from some esters of glycerol (an alcohol containing three $-OH$ groups) and high relative molecular mass carboxylic acids. For example, beef and mutton fat reacting with aqueous sodium hydroxide produce glycerol and the sodium salt of the acid (soap). This process is called saponification.

Terylene is a polyester, i.e. it consists of acid and alcohol units linked together in a chain. Each time an alcohol molecule links with an acid molecule to form an ester-type linkage, a molecule of water is also produced. This process is thus known as condensation polymerization. Organic acids will also combine with amines (compounds containing the $-NH_2$ group), and again a molecule of water is produced each time these molecules join. In this case the resulting chain polymer is called nylon.

The amino acids contain two functional groups, $-NH_2$ and $-COOH$, and proteins are formed by some amino acids linking into chains. Although nylon and proteins both contain

peptide linkages, $-CO-NH-$ or

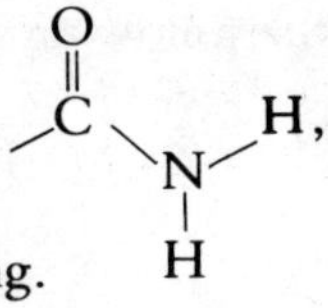

$$\underset{\underset{\overset{|}{H}}{N}}{\overset{\overset{O}{\|}}{C}}H,$$ one is better

for clothing and the other for eating.

Questions

1 The formula of sodium ethanoate is CH_3COONa. The charge on the ethanoate ion is thus

   A -2
   B -1
   C 0
   D $+1$
   E $+2$

2 Which of the following reagents may be used to convert a hydrocarbon into a soapless detergent?

   A   sodium hydroxide
   B   concentrated sulphuric acid
   C   a catalyst
   D   concentrated sulphuric acid, followed by sodium hydroxide
   E   sodium hydroxide, followed by concentrated sulphuric acid

3 When ethanol is burnt completely in air the products are

   A   steam and carbon monoxide.
   B   steam and carbon dioxide.
   C   steam and carbon.
   D   carbon and carbon monoxide.
   E   carbon and carbon dioxide.

4 Which of the following does *not* react with phosphorus pentachloride?

   A   ethane-1,2-diol
   B   ethanol
   C   ethanoic acid
   D   ethane
   E   water

5   Which of the following is *not* polymeric?

    A   Terylene
    B   nylon
    C   starch
    D   ethene
    E   protein

6   The atoms in methane are arranged

    A   cubically.
    B   octahedrally.
    C   tetrahedrally.
    D   squarely.
    E   in a circle.

7   Which of the following substances is *not* produced by the distillation of petroleum?

    A   ethanol
    B   butane
    C   paraffin
    D   petrol
    E   naphtha

8   Which of the following cannot be made in *one* step from ethene?

    A   ethane-1,2-diol
    B   1,2-dibromoethane
    C   ethane
    D   methanol
    E   2-bromoethanol

9   The main component of natural gas is

    A   oxygen.
    B   nitrogen.
    C   methane.
    D   carbon dioxide.
    E   argon.

10   Which of the following substances is that of an isomer of
     butane

```
        H  H  H  H
        |  |  |  |
   H—C—C—C—C—H    ?
        |  |  |  |
        H  H  H  H
```

```
        H  H  H
        |  |  |
A   H—C— C— C—H
        |  |  |
        H  H  |
             H—C—H
                |
                H
```

```
        H           H
        |           |
B   H—C           C—H
        |           |
        H—C—H  H—C—H
        |           |
        H           H
```

```
     H
     |
C  H—C—H        H
     |          |
   H—C          C—H
     |          |
     H        H—C—H
                |
                H
```

```
        H  H  H
        |  |  |
D  H—C—C—C—H
        |  |  |
        |  H  H
      H—C—H
        |
        H
```

```
     H  H  H
     |  |  |
E  H—C—C—C—H
     |  |  |
     H  |  H
        |
     H—C—H
        |
        H
```

11 Which of the following organic compounds, represented by their structures, is an ester?

```
        H  H
        |  |       H
A  H—C—C—O         |
        |  |  \    C—C—H
        H  H   \C  |
             O//   H
```

```
        H  H
        |  |
B  H—C—C—O—H
        |  |
        H  H
```

```
        H  H  H  H
        |  |  |  |
C  H—C—C—C—C—H
        |  |  |  |
        H  H  H  H
```

```
        H
        |        O
D  H—C—C//
        |        \
        H         O—H
```

```
        H
        |        O
E  H—C—C//
        |        \
        H          H
```

12 Which of the following reagents will convert ethene into ethane-1,2-diol?

 A water
 B concentrated sulphuric acid
 C sodium hydroxide solution
 D ethanol
 E alkaline potassium manganate(VII) solution

13 Which reaction, represented by one of the following equations, is a substitution reaction?

 A $CH_4 + Cl_2 \rightarrow CH_3Cl + HCl$

 B $CH_4 + 2O_2 \rightarrow CO_2 + 2H_2O$

 C $C_2H_5OH + 3O_2 \rightarrow 2CO_2 + 3H_2O$

 D $CH_3COOH + NaOH \rightarrow CH_3COONa + H_2O$

 E $CH_3COOH + C_2H_5OH \rightarrow CH_3COOC_2H_5$
    $+ H_2O$

14 Which of the following substances will react with warm sodium hydroxide solution?

 A ethyl ethanoate
 B ethene
 C ethanol
 D ethane
 E ethane-1,2-diol

15 Which reaction, represented by one of the following equations, is an addition reaction?

 A $CH_3COOH + C_2H_5OH \rightarrow CH_3COOC_2H_5$
    $+ H_2O$

 B $C_2H_5OH + PCl_5 \rightarrow C_2H_5Cl + POCl_3 + HCl$

 C $2C_2H_5OH + 2Na \rightarrow 2C_2H_5ONa + H_2$

 D $C_2H_4 + H_2 \rightarrow C_2H_6$

 E $CH_3CH_2CH_2CH_3 \rightarrow CH_3CH(CH_3)_2$

Select the appropriate response from the following types of reaction for *questions 16–20.*

A polymerization
B esterification
C combustion
D cracking
E substitution

Which of these responses *best* describes

16 the conversion of ethanoic acid and ethanol into ethyl ethanoate?

17 the oxidation of ethanol into carbon dioxide and water?

18 the conversion of chloroethene (vinyl chloride) into a plastic solid?

19 the conversion of decane into octane and ethene?

20 the conversion of ethanol into chloroethane.

Select the appropriate response from the following processes for *questions 21–25.*

A hydrogenation
B hydration
C fermentation
D distillation
E hydrolysis

Which of these responses *best* describes

21 converting ethene into ethane?

22 making ethanol from carbohydrates?

23 making an ester into an alcohol and an acid?

24 converting ethene into ethanol?

25 converting an oil into a fat?

The Periodic Table

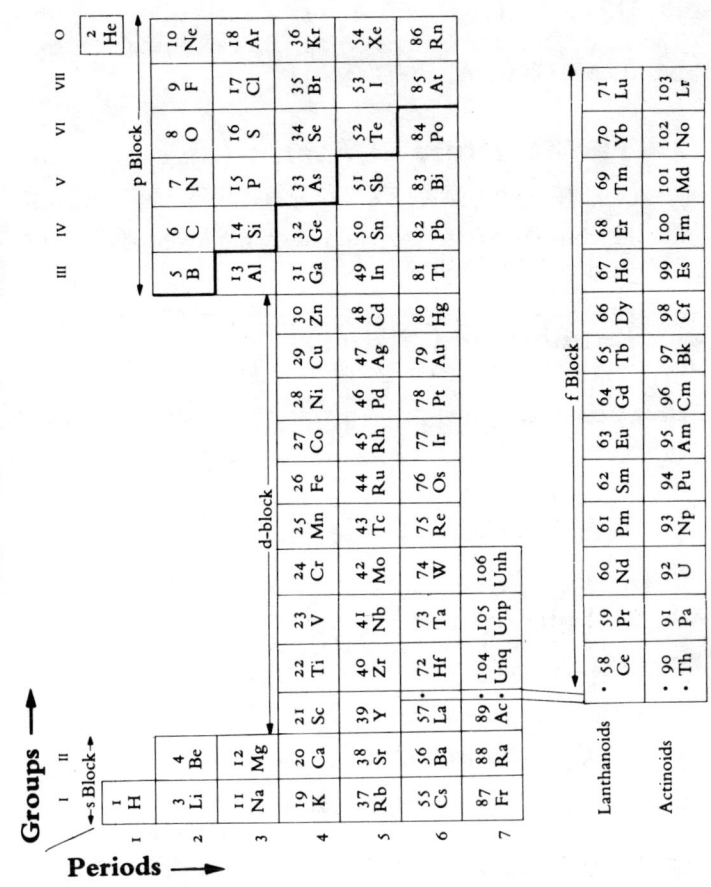

Groups →

Periods →

Answers

1 Classification (page 1)

1. C, 2. D, 3. A, 4. A, 5. B, 6. C, 7. E, 8. A, 9. A,
10. D, 11. E, 12. D, 13. E, 14. C, 15. B, 16. A, 17. A,
18. E, 19. B, 20. E, 21. C, 22. E, 23. A, 24. D, 25. C,
26. A, 27. C, 28. A, 29. D, 30. D.

2 The Structure of Atoms (page 9)

1. D, 2. B, 3. C, 4. C, 5. C, 6. B, 7. E, 8. C, 9. A,
10. D, 11. A, 12. E, 13. C, 14. D, 15. B, 16. C, 17. A,
18. E, 19. D, 20. B, 21. A, 22. C, 23. E, 24. D, 25. E.

3 Bonding and Structure (page 16)

1. E, 2. D, 3. D, 4. A, 5. E, 6. E, 7. D, 8. B, 9. E,
10. A, 11. D, 12. B, 13. E, 14. A, 15. C, 16. D, 17. A,
18. D, 19. C, 20. E, 21. B, 22. E, 23. A, 24. C, 25. C,

4 The Periodic Table (page 25)

1. D, 2. D, 3. E, 4. C, 5. C, 6. D, 7. C, 8. D, 9. D,
10. A, 11. A, 12. C, 13. B, 14. B, 15. C, 16. A, 17. D,
18. C, 19. E, 20. B, 21. A, 22. C, 23. D, 24. C, 25. D,
26. E, 27. B, 28. A, 29. E.

5 Redox Reactions (page 33)

1. A, 2. A, 3. B, 4. B, 5. C, 6. E, 7. B, 8. D, 9. D,
10. E, 11. B, 12. D, 13. D, 14. A, 15. D, 16. D, 17. A,
18. B, 19. B, 20. A, 21. A, 22. D, 23. E, 24. C, 25. E.

6 Acids, Bases and Salts (page 42)

1. A, 2. D, 3. A, 4. C, 5. E, 6. B, 7. A, 8. D, 9. D,
10. A, 11. E, 12. A, 13. B, 14. D, 15. D, 16. E, 17. A,
18. C, 19. D, 20. B, 21. D, 22. C, 23. B, 24. A, 25. A,
26. D, 27. A, 28. B, 29. E, 30. C.

7 The Mole Concept (page 52)

1. E, 2. A, 3. D, 4. D, 5. C, 6. A, 7. B, 8. C, 9. D,
10. E, 11. A, 12. A, 13. B, 14. B, 15. D, 16. E, 17. D,
18. B, 19. E, 20. B, 21. D, 22. C, 23. C, 24. B, 25. A.

8 Energy Changes and Rates of Reaction (page 63)

1. E, 2. A, 3. C, 4. B, 5. B, 6. D, 7. C, 8. B, 9. D,
10. C, 11. C, 12. A, 13. D, 14. C, 15. D, 16. A, 17. B,
18. C, 19. E, 20. B, 21. A, 22. D, 23. B, 24. C, 25. E.

9 Air, Water and the Environment (page 75)

1. B, 2. C, 3. D, 4. A, 5. B, 6. C, 7. B, 8. B, 9. B,
10. A, 11. D, 12. E, 13. A, 14. C, 15. C, 16. C, 17. B,
18. E, 19. D, 20. A, 21. C, 22. C, 23. E, 24. D, 25. C.

10 Metals (page 87)

1. A, 2. D, 3. B, 4. A, 5. B, 6. A, 7. D, 8. A, 9. D,
10. D, 11. B, 12. B, 13. C, 14. B, 15. D, 16. E, 17. D,
18. C, 19. B, 20. A, 21. E, 22. A, 23. D, 24. C, 25. B.

11 Non-metals (page 98)

1. A, 2. B, 3. A, 4. B, 5. B, 6. E, 7. B, 8. D, 9. D,
10. A, 11. C, 12. A, 13. B, 14. B, 15. D, 16. B, 17. E,
18. A, 19. C, 20. D, 21. A, 22. D, 23. B, 24. C, 25. C.

12 Organic Chemistry (page 110)

1. B, 2. D, 3. B, 4. D, 5. D, 6. C, 7. A, 8. D, 9. C,
10. E, 11. A, 12. E, 13. A, 14. A, 15. D, 16. B, 17. C,
18. A, 19. D, 20. E, 21. A, 22. C, 23. E, 24. B, 25. A.

Data for Calculations

The following values should be used as appropriate for calculations.

Molar volume at standard
temperature and pressure $= 22.4 \, dm^3 \, mol^{-1}$
Avogadro constant $\quad = 6.02 \times 10^{23} \, mol^{-1}$
Faraday constant $\quad = 96\,500$ coulomb mol^{-1}
$1000 \, cm^3 = 1 \, dm^3$ (litre)

Relative Atomic Masses

Aluminium	27	Magnesium	~~25~~ 24
Argon	40	Manganese	55
Barium	137	Mercury	201
Boron	11	Nickel	59
Bromine	80	Nitrogen	14
Calcium	40	Oxygen	16
Carbon	12	Phosphorus	31
Chlorine	35.5	Potassium	39
Chromium	52	Silicon	28
Copper	64	Silver	108
Fluorine	19	Sodium	23
Helium	4	Sulphur	32
Hydrogen	1	Tin	119
Iodine	127	Titanium	48
Iron	56	Vanadium	51
Lead	207	Xenon	131
		Zinc	65